NURSES MIND YOUR BUSINESS

THE HEALTHCARE ENTREPRENEUR'S PLAYBOOK

by
Dr. Nancy A. Hurlock,
DNP, AGPCNP-BC

Copyright © 2025 by Nancy A. Hurlock

All rights reserved. No part of this book may be reproduced or transmitted in any form without written permission from the author, except for brief quotations used in reviews or educational contexts.

Self-Published
ISBN: 979-8-218-77017-4

Printed in the United States

Disclaimer:

This book is intended for informational and educational purposes only. The author and publisher are not responsible for any outcomes related to the application of the information provided. Readers are encouraged to consult qualified professionals before implementing any strategies discussed.

Table of Contents

Acknowledgments v

Introduction vii

    Chapter 1: Who This Book Is For 1

    Chapter 2: A New Reality 5

    Chapter 3: It Starts In Your Mind: The REAL Barrier You Face 15

    Chapter 4: The One Thing That Will Make or Break Your Business Success 29

    Chapter 5: The Foundation - Building Your Business Plan with Your "Why" at the Center 41

    Chapter 6: The Core Mechanism: Choosing Your Business Model 49

    Chapter 7: Creating Your Business: Legal, Licensing & Logistics.... 57

    Chapter 8: Preparing to See Clients: Where Preparation Meets Purpose 69

    Chapter 9: The Critical Component: Finding and Serving Your First Clients 77

    Chapter 10: Serving Your First Clients 85

    Chapter 11: Seeing What's Missing, Creating What's Next 93

Conclusion: Lead with Passion. Serve with Purpose 109

References 113

My Journey 115

Acknowledgements

I must begin by acknowledging how truly blessed I am to be surrounded by a support system that uplifts, inspires, and motivates me to pursue the desires of my heart.

First and foremost, I give thanks to God. Without Him, none of this would be possible. He has gifted me with discernment, strength, and unwavering perseverance even when the journey felt impossible. My confidence is rooted not in my own abilities, but entirely in His grace and guidance.

To my parents, Frederick and Zenia Raymond, thank you for being an example of what hard work, dedication, and faith can achieve. You instilled in me the value of education and the belief that anything is possible with determination.

To my husband, Dr. William "Gary" Hurlock, for over 30 years (*and counting*), you have been my rock, my partner, and my constant source of strength.

To my three beautiful children, Amanda, Adrianna, and Andrew, you are my heartbeats. Through your eyes, I've learned to see the world with wonder and endless possibilities, unbound by limitation or fear.

To my siblings, my family, and my dearest friends, I love each of you deeply. Thank you for embracing me fully, for accepting me as I am, for pushing me forward, and for cheering me on every step of the way.

From the bottom of my heart—**thank you.**

Introduction

What if the solution your patients have been waiting for… is you?

As a nurse, I quickly realized that many of us are conditioned to wait for permission before we act. We bring our expertise to every situation, yet we are rarely empowered to make critical decisions that create real change. I learned this the hard way until I stepped into the world of entrepreneurship and discovered a truth that changed everything: in business, you are the decision-maker. You are the answer to the problem.

In 2018, I launched my own healthcare practice with a simple but powerful mission to meet people where they were and deliver compassionate care when no one else would. I became the only Nurse Practitioner in Southeast Georgia operating a solo practice focused exclusively on house calls and home-based primary care. My goal was never to be flashy; it was to serve those who were too often overlooked by traditional healthcare systems.

Covering more than 400 miles as a solo provider meant long days, sleepless nights, and moments when I questioned whether the work was sustainable. But each time I walked through a patient's door, I was reminded exactly why I chose this path. Every challenge became an opportunity. Every mile brought me closer to someone who needed care, and that made every sacrifice worth it.

Eventually, I made the decision to merge my practice to expand its reach beyond Southeast Georgia. Today, our team serves a broader region, carrying forward the mission of caring for individuals affected by chronic illness and the social factors that influence health. As I transition from CEO and day-to-day operator to Founder, I hold deep pride and gratitude for the communities that welcomed me, the patients and families who placed their trust in me, and the colleagues and supporters who believed in this work from the very beginning.

To those considering starting a similar practice, you can do this. I began with nothing but a vision, a calling, and the courage to show up. You do not need to wait for permission. In entrepreneurship, you have the power to lead, to innovate, and to turn your passion into a purpose-driven business.

This journey has taught me that if you stay rooted in your mission and guided by your values, everything else will follow. Even when the road feels uncertain, believe in what is possible, because the mission continues. And the world is still waiting for you.

Chapter 1

Who This Book Is For

If you're holding this book, there's a reason. Maybe you're a nurse, physician, therapist, social worker, or some other kind of healthcare provider who's felt that *pull*, the urge to do something different. Something bold. Maybe even something of your own.

This book is for you.

It's for the healthcare professional who's spent years serving others and now feels a fire to serve in a new way through a business born from passion, purpose, and a desire to fill the gaps that traditional systems leave behind.

It's especially for those of you who care for older adults, who feel a strong sense of purpose in community-based care, or who know deep down that we can do better by the people aging in our communities. If you've spent time at the bedside, in homes, in clinics, or in underserved communities, and asked yourself, *"Why isn't this easier?"* or *"Why does this keep happening?"*, you're in the right place.

But let me be clear: this book isn't just for healthcare providers focused on geriatrics or home care.

This book is for anyone in the healing space who wants to launch a business and build something that reflects their vision and values.

Some of you reading this might already have a business idea. Maybe it's scribbled in a notebook, saved in your phone, or fully mapped out with spreadsheets and prototypes. You've been dreaming and planning, but you're looking for clarity or confirmation that now is the time.

Others might not have a business idea yet, but something inside you knows you're not meant to spend your entire career operating inside someone else's box. You're entrepreneurial minded even if you haven't said those words out loud yet.

This book is for you.

It's for the bold dreamer and the quiet questioner. It's for the clinician who's already taken steps toward business ownership, and for the one who's still working 12-hour shifts wondering if this could really be possible.

You don't need a business degree to be here.
You don't need an investor.
You don't even need an exact blueprint.

What you need is openness to learn, the courage to think differently, and the willingness to believe that the impact you were born to make might actually begin with *you*.

So, if you've ever thought:

"I want to do something meaningful."
"I'm ready to step outside the traditional system."
"There has to be a better way to serve the people I care about."
"Could I really build something that matters?"

Then yes, this book was written for you.

Whether you're looking to launch a house call practice, start a consulting firm, open a wellness clinic, create a mobile service, or design something the world hasn't seen yet, this journey is yours to take.

And I'm here to walk it with you.

Chapter 2

A New Reality

Before I ever called myself an entrepreneur, I spent over sixteen years in home and community health, up close to the realities many people never see. I cared for older adults in their most vulnerable moments, often homebound, alone, and forgotten by a system that wasn't built for them. I saw what happened when people couldn't get their medications, couldn't access medical equipment, or couldn't make it to their primary care provider because they physically couldn't leave their home.

Over time, I kept asking the same question:

Why doesn't the provider just go to them?

You might know that feeling too, the frustration of seeing the same broken patterns and wondering why no one is stepping in to fix them. That frustration is often the spark of entrepreneurship. For many of us, it starts with a question, a gut feeling, or an idea that won't go away. And here's the thing: not everyone acts on it.

But I did.

On June 12, 2018, I officially launched my house call practice. I had no investors, no big-name partners, just a deep conviction that *this* is what I was meant to do. At the time, I was the only Nurse Practitioner in Southeast Georgia operating a solo practice focused exclusively on house calls and home-based primary care.

What started as a simple mission to bring care directly to the people who needed it most grew into something much bigger: a movement.

That's how entrepreneurship often begins. You see a need no one is meeting. You feel a pull you can't ignore. And eventually, the desire to create something that matters becomes stronger than your fear of failure.

My model was simple: *meet people where they are.* Literally. I built this practice for seniors and homebound patients who were left behind by traditional healthcare. I covered a 400-mile radius, just me, my car, and a calling.

It wasn't easy. Not even close. There were long days, late nights, and plenty of moments where quitting would've been the easier option. But every challenge brought me back to the *why*, the patient on the other side of the door. The person who had been waiting far too long for someone to show up.

I felt that someone was me. I saw the need, I saw the unbeaten path, and I knew I had to act.

If you're reading this because you're thinking of building something, starting something, or launching something; hear me clearly:

You don't need permission.
You don't need to have it all figured out.
You need to *believe that you can be the one who answers the question nobody else is answering.*

That was me.

Like many nurses and healthcare professionals, I had been conditioned to wait for approval. We're trained to follow the rules, not break the mold. And we are rarely exposed to entrepreneurship or business education. But eventually, I got tired of waiting. I realized I didn't have to keep asking *why doesn't someone do something?* Because I could be that someone.

I gained business knowledge. I took the leap. And I launched.

I built the model. I drove the miles. I met the patients where they were.

When I launched my practice in 2018, I was genuinely excited about bringing home-based primary care to patients who needed it most. I believed deeply in the value of meeting people where they were, literally. I tried every marketing method I could think of, word of mouth, printed materials, door-to-door outreach. I approached other healthcare organizations and medical practices, hoping they would share my excitement about the return of house calls.

But to my surprise, the idea was not immediately embraced. Instead, I was met with closed doors and polite rejections that stung more than I expected.

I would spend hours preparing for meetings, only to have them canceled at the last moment without explanation. On the rare occasions I made it into the room, I would speak to a sea of distracted faces, eyes fixed on phones or laptops, as if my words were background noise. Calls went unanswered, emails disappeared into the void. No matter how clearly I painted the vision, it felt like no one was ready to see what I saw.

So, I decided to move forward anyway, on my own.

Thankfully, I was not completely alone. I had a mentor in another part of Georgia who was already providing home-based care and who generously shared her experience and wisdom. I will forever be grateful to Patricia Gray-Smith, MSN, APRN, FNP-C, for openly offering resources, guidance, and practical advice on how to get started, while always remaining just a phone call away. Her support made all the difference for me and highlighted how incredibly valuable the RIGHT mentorship is when you're starting a new venture. I also sought training opportunities across the country, connecting with others who were pioneering this model in their own communities. I traveled to courses that taught everything from launching a practice to managing the technical and business aspects of healthcare ownership. When travel was not possible, I made the most of online training sessions to continue learning and building my skills.

And then, the pandemic happened.

The world shut down. Everything we knew as "normal" changed, including how healthcare was delivered. The very population I had long identified as underserved older adults and homebound individuals became even more isolated, even more vulnerable.

And then… my phone started ringing. My inbox overflowed.

Everyone remembered the nurse practitioner who was willing to see patients at home.

Assisted living communities, unable to let residents leave for care, suddenly needed immediate solutions. I mean immediate. Medications still had to be managed. Therapy still needed to be provided. Healthcare didn't stop and now, it had to come to them.

While everyone and everything stopped, I was on the go. I put more miles on my vehicle than ever before, and the areas I covered continued to expand. My days began and ended with responding to the needs of individuals whose challenges went far beyond traditional healthcare. Families were struggling with the weight of isolation, while patients grew increasingly anxious and, quite honestly, depressed. I often found myself acting as a bridge between patients and their families, since the community teams where they lived were already stretched thin. For many, we became a connection to what they considered the outside world. I could never have predicted that my practice would take this turn; but it did. And without question, I knew this was a calling.

The problem I had been trying to solve all along finally became clear to everyone else. **What was once considered a niche idea was now *necessary*.**

What had been a quiet movement became a vital response.

The answer had always been there; we just needed a new lens to see it.

I'm forever grateful to the communities, patients, and families who opened their doors to me and believed in this work long before it had a title, a logo, or a budget.

If you're standing at the edge of your own idea, wondering if you're crazy for wanting to do things differently, let me tell you: *you're not crazy.* You might just be an entrepreneur. And if you are, welcome. You're in the right place.

Let's Go Back to the Beginning

Let me take you behind the scenes into the reality of what it looked like to build something from the ground up. The long nights. The full calendar. The dreams scribbled in notebooks or in my case, "a three-ring binder". The moments of clarity tucked between school pickups and work meetings.

Before I saw my first patient as the founder of a home-based primary care practice in June 2018, there was a journey. A long one. And it wasn't always glamorous.

When I opened my practice, Beyond Health Group, I wasn't doing so from a place of excess or ease. I was doing so as a wife. As a mother of three incredible children ages 9, 8 and 7 at the time. As someone working full-time, managing a demanding career in healthcare leadership. As someone pursuing advanced education. I was living life at full volume, juggling responsibilities while fiercely protecting my vision of what could be.

I had already spent over sixteen years in the home healthcare field, serving in various roles from registered nurse field clinician to Clinical Director, and eventually as an Area Director overseeing multiple agencies across Southeast Georgia. These roles didn't just build my resume; they built my resolve. I witnessed firsthand the gaps in care, especially for older adults living in rural and underserved areas. I saw the patients being missed, too frail to travel, too complex to be served in traditional models, too often forgotten.

And I began to imagine a different way.

I brought that vision to boardrooms, to leadership teams, to decision-makers. I advocated for a model that brought healthcare into the home, one that could reduce hospitalizations, ease suffering, and meet patients where they were.

But what I heard in return was silence. No traction. No interest. No doors opening.

At the time, I shared this idea with others, believing they were the ones qualified to make it happen and that I was simply offering the concept. I introduced myself as the nurse practitioner who could see patients unable to leave their homes. It never occurred to me that I might be the one to start or even open such a practice myself.

I kept thinking, *no one sees the value in this model? How could that be possible?* To me it was as clear as day.

I soon realized it wasn't that no one saw this as a viable option; it was that we often get stuck in doing things the way they've always been done, hesitant to challenge the system or explore new possibilities.

That silence could have stopped me, but instead, it pushed me forward. I embraced change. I embraced uncertainty. I stopped asking for permission and started carving my own path. As I've shared before: *I didn't just think outside the box, I built my own.*

And that decision didn't come without sacrifice. There were long nights filled with coursework, first for my master's degree as I worked toward becoming a nurse practitioner, and later for my doctoral program. Mornings that started before the sun. Moments when I questioned if I could keep all the plates spinning. But I did. I leaned on my support system who believed in me and in this vision even when the road ahead wasn't clear.

I'm often asked how I "did it all." The honest answer? **I didn't do it all at once and I didn't do it alone.**

MIND YOUR BUSINESS TRUTH #1

Here's the truth: I didn't share everything with my support system.

Sometimes, you have to move in silence. While the world is sleeping, you're grinding. While others are out socializing, you're quietly putting in the work to build the life you envision.

That was my reality. When I decided to return to school to pursue my doctorate, I had already earned my master's degree, launched my business, and was working four PRN jobs. Saying, "Guess what, I'm going back to school," would have sounded insane to most. But I wasn't crazy, I was focused. I had a vision. I had goals. And I was determined to see them through.

I didn't keep my journey private because my family didn't support me or wanted to see me succeed. They absolutely did. But I knew this path would raise questions. Why take on something so demanding, so exhausting, with everything else already on my plate? I didn't want them to worry. I didn't want to explain a vision that only I was meant to understand at the time.

So, I kept it to myself. I committed, studied, sacrificed and completed my entire doctoral journey without telling my family. They didn't know until the very end.

Because sometimes, when your purpose is loud, your process has to be quiet.

What I did do, was commit to taking one step at a time. I often told myself to take it "one second at a time". I trusted the process, even when it was slow. I stayed rooted in my purpose, even when it was hard. I gave myself permission to fall as long as I kept getting back up.

And I kept my eye on the people I was called to serve.

This wasn't just about building a business. It was about creating a solution to a problem that had been ignored for too long. It was about being the kind of provider I wished existed for so many patients and families I had met over the years. It was about leading with compassion and creating a model of care that put people first.

As I share this with you now, I want to remind you of something:

You don't have to wait until life is perfect to begin.

You don't have to have every answer before you take the first step.

You just have to believe that your vision matters and that your voice, your effort, and your passion can create something that didn't exist before.

I say this to you not just as a business owner or clinician, but as someone who has lived the juggling act. Who has studied with little ones tugging at my sleeve, school papers spread across the table, snacks in hand, and dinner simmering on the stove. Who has built a practice between PTA meetings and patient charting. Who understands the pressure of trying to do it all and the quiet strength that comes from doing what matters anyway.

This chapter is just a reminder that the road is not always straight but it's always worth walking.

So, before we dive back into the next phase of building your business, take a breath. Acknowledge the life you're living while you build. And trust that your journey, however messy, nonlinear, or complicated is preparing you to lead something extraordinary.

Chapter 3

It Starts In Your Mind: The REAL Barrier You Face

Before we go any further, let's talk about the *real* reason so many brilliant, capable healthcare professionals; people just like you never take the leap into entrepreneurship.

It's not a lack of skill.
It's not a lack of opportunity.
It's not even a lack of ideas. *(Trust me, if you have an entrepreneurial spirit, your biggest challenge will probably be having too many ideas!)*

More often than not, *it's mindset*.

In healthcare, we are conditioned to work within structure. We follow protocols. We prioritize precision. We wait for approval. We lean into stability. That mindset serves us well in clinical environments, but it can unintentionally build walls when we try to break into the entrepreneurial world.

The business world is *different*.

The business world doesn't always offer structure.

It doesn't ask permission.
It moves faster.
It rewards boldness.

It rewards courage, adaptability, and speed over perfection. And it doesn't wait for you to feel "ready."

But the truth is as healthcare providers aspiring to be entrepreneurs, there is an invisible weight we carry. When I first considered starting a business, I was weighed down by every internal and external obstacle you could imagine. Self-doubt. Fear of failure. Guilt about dividing my time between patients, family, and this "wild" new idea I couldn't shake. And yes, the whispers; sometimes loud, of people who didn't understand why I'd want to leave the comfort of a reliable paycheck for something so uncertain.

And let's be honest: as healthcare professionals, we're *not* trained to think like entrepreneurs. We are trained to *serve*, not *sell*. We are told to *document*, not *dream*. We are often taught that clinical mastery is the pinnacle, but what if it's just one step in your journey?

I had to learn that building something new, a practice, a company, a movement, starts not with a business plan, but with a belief system.

A belief that:

- You are capable of more.
- You can make an impact and income.
- You can serve your community without sacrificing your sanity or your worth.

Instead of letting those hurdles stop me, I decided to meet them head-on.

Let me walk you through some of the most common ones, and how I tackled them.

The First Real Hurdle: Rewriting the Script

Shifting your mindset isn't a one-time decision. It's a process. It's catching the quiet thoughts that say, *"Who am I to do this?"* and responding with, *"Who am I not to?"*

It's recognizing that fear doesn't mean stop, it means *this matters*.

It's redefining failure, not as a reason to retreat, but as a tool for refinement.

It's moving from:

"I don't know how,"
to
"I'm willing to figure it out."

Because here's what I've learned: the hurdles that appear to be "out there", the funding, the systems, the logistics, are often easier to navigate than the ones in our own minds.

And once you break through *that* barrier? Everything else starts to move.

Let me tell you how this played out for me. When I first had the idea of starting my own home-based healthcare practice, I was still working full-time, raising three young children, and finishing graduate school. I had every reason to wait. I didn't have a business background, but I had clinical expertise and a solid understanding of clinical operations, and I leaned into that. I didn't have investors or a team. All I had was a vision, a lot of determination, and quite frankly a deep dislike for losing.

I remember sitting at my kitchen table one evening, insurance credentialing forms spread out in front of me because I was applying on my own. I couldn't afford to hire a company to handle the process for me. My children were playing in the background, and I thought to myself, *"You're crazy for even thinking about this right now."*

But something kept nudging me forward. I couldn't shake the belief that I was supposed to serve in a different way that my community needed care delivered beyond the walls of a traditional clinic. That someone had to start. And maybe that someone was me.

So, I started small. No office, no staff, just a laptop, a phone, and a determination to figure it out as I went.

I still remember my first patient visit under my own business. It was more than just a professional milestone, it was personal. I had reviewed the care plan a dozen times, double and triple checking everything, nervous about whether the family would trust me, whether I had made the right decision stepping out on my own.

But it was also exciting.

I was finally transitioning the deep knowledge I had developed as a registered nurse in home health into my role as an Adult-Gerontology Nurse Practitioner. As I walked into their home and provided care; on my terms, with my values, I felt something shift.

In that moment, I knew.

I had started to break through the biggest hurdle: my own doubt. And with every step I took, I laid the foundation for something bigger, a practice built on compassion, clinical excellence, and integrity. That first visit marked the beginning of a mission rooted in both passion and purpose.

And that's what I want for you.

You don't have to have it all figured out. You just have to start with what you have, where you are.

The Second Real Hurdle: Overcoming the Funding Challenge

Start with what you have. That's what I had to do.

You don't need $100,000 in the bank to start a healthcare business. What you *do* need is creativity, resourcefulness, and the courage to start small; and to start now.

When I launched my practice, I didn't have a private office, a dedicated team, or a big budget. I self-funded everything using my personal savings. There were no grants, no investors, no angel donors, just me, my vision, and a clear understanding of what truly mattered: delivering compassionate, accessible care to those who needed it most.

Believe me, I tried to secure funding. I reached out to banks, submitted applications, and explored small business grants. I remember sitting through meetings with bank managers, explaining my vision and presenting projections that demonstrated minimal, low-risk funding needs, yet nothing came of it. The return calls never came. The silence was deafening. Meanwhile, others I met at networking events would boast about large lines of credit extended to them, often without the same qualifications, years of experience, or progress in establishing their business as I had. It was, quite frankly, discouraging. I had to maintain my composure during those conversations while battling a sickening feeling in my gut. At that moment, I faced a choice: wait for someone else to believe in me or bet on myself. I chose to move forward on my own.

Instead of renting expensive office space, I found a co-working space and signed up for a basic "Hot Desk" membership for just $75 a month. This gave me access to shared tables, Wi-Fi, and a professional business address. It was simple, affordable, and exactly what I needed to get started without unnecessary overhead.

I didn't rush to hire staff or build a flashy website. Instead, I prioritized building a transparent online presence. As a provider entering people's homes, I knew trust was everything. Patients and families needed to easily verify who I was, see my credentials, and feel confident in my qualifications before I even knocked on their door.

I didn't invest in fancy branding or costly software at the outset. In fact, my children were the ones who named my company and even helped design the logo. It was simple, heartfelt, and deeply meaningful proof that starting small doesn't mean starting without purpose or passion. My son, yes, even at that young age, was my IT guy. Fortunately for me, he had (and still has) a natural knack for technology, always ready to help me set up my devices and troubleshoot any software challenges. My daughters pitched in too, helping me organize paperwork, set up my calendar, and manage the many administrative tasks that kept me organized and focused.

From day one, I focused on what mattered most: connecting with patients, providing excellent care, and building relationships. Everything else could grow from there.

Here's the truth about funding, and it's one that every aspiring entrepreneur needs to hear:

If you wait until everything is perfectly lined up and fully financed, you'll be waiting forever.

Start with what you have and grow from there. Take a deep inventory of your resources, your skills, your connections, your time and begin right where you are. Do the research. Explore what tools and support systems already exist. Learn what you can manage yourself, and outsource strategically and only when necessary, keeping your budget in mind.

A lean, intentional start allows you to focus on what truly matters: delivering value and building trust with your community.

You don't need a big budget to make a big impact, you need clarity, creativity, and unwavering commitment.

You don't need to "look" successful to *be* successful. Keep your overhead low. Use the tools at your disposal, many of which are free or affordable and be intentional with every dollar you spend.

Your energy, your resourcefulness, and your determination are far more valuable than any early capital you might raise.

You are your first investor.

Believe in your mission enough to bet on yourself.

And trust me when you do that, others will see your commitment, and they will follow.

Starting small is not a limitation; it's a strategic advantage. It teaches you to be nimble, to prioritize, and to grow sustainably one meaningful step at a time.

So, take that step today. Build from your passion, your purpose, and the resources you already have. Your future business and the people you'll serve are counting on it.

> *"If you wait until everything is perfectly funded, you'll be waiting forever. Instead, start with what you have, and build as you grow. You are your first investor*

The Third Real Hurdle: It's Who You Know—and Who You Don't: Building the Right Team from Day One

When you're starting a business, it's important to know who you need and who you don't.

In any business, there are two types of team members:

- Revenue producers
- Revenue consumers

Simply put, there are team members who directly drive revenue - revenue producers. Then there are those whose day-to-day tasks do not directly generate revenue for the business - revenue consumers. Each one is important but knowing the difference is important as you start your business.

In healthcare, the healthcare provider is the revenue producer, the one whose work directly generates income because as they see their patients, revenue is generated. Reimbursement is generated as a direct result of their actions.

That distinction gave me a unique advantage when it came time to launch my own practice.

MIND YOUR BUSINESS TRUTH #2

Let me take a moment to emphasize this: as Advanced Practice Providers, you must know your worth. Understand the value you bring to the table. The work you do and the care you provide every day directly contribute to the success of healthcare organizations and improve the quality of life for countless patients, their families, and caregivers.

Before opening my business, I spent years in home health care. During that time, I wasn't just leading, I was learning every aspect of the operation. I made it a point to sit in every seat. I learned about intake. I handled credentialing and insurance verification. I understood scheduling, compliance, and how to keep things running behind the scenes. That was the kind of leader I was. I believed in all hands on deck and I never saw myself above or below any tasks. Not because I knew then what was to come, but because it was always in my nature to be a team player. Whenever we were short-staffed, I'd step in and fill the gap never realizing how valuable that experience would be later.

That hands on experience became one of my greatest assets. So, when I opened my practice as a Nurse Practitioner who had also served as a Clinical Manager, Area Director, and had been deeply involved in clinical operations I didn't need to hire anyone in the beginning. I brought those skills with me.

I did the intake. I verified the insurance. I scheduled the appointments.

And after all of that I still went out and saw the patients.

Now, if you don't have that level of operational knowledge or experience, that's okay but it does mean you'll need to hire someone to manage those critical administrative tasks while you focus on patient care. These roles, while essential, are considered revenue consumers, they don't directly generate income, but your practice can't function without them.

That's why your first hire needs to be a strategic one, ideally someone who is cross-trained, skilled, and adaptable enough to support the evolving needs of a growing practice.

My children were often in the car with me when I took calls for the practice. They'd overhear me talking to vendors, patients, or partners and eventually ask, "Mommy, why do you always say we? It's just you."

I'd smile and simply respond, "It's okay, kiddos."

What they didn't understand then was that "we" wasn't about how many people were working with me at the time, it was about the vision. I spoke in "we" because I was building something bigger than myself. I was laying the foundation for a business that would one day have a team, a culture, and a collective mission. I used "we" because I was thinking long-term, about the company I was growing into, not just the solo effort in that moment.

"We" was a declaration of faith in the future.

And that vision? It's unfolding every day.

In the beginning, I did everything myself, intake, billing, scheduling, even marketing. And that was okay. That season taught me exactly what my business needed and what I could eventually delegate or outsource.

Thankfully, my years of experience in clinical operations ranging from working as a field registered nurse to serving as a clinical manager, branch director, and eventually area director had prepared me well. Each of those roles exposed me to different aspects of healthcare operations and helped me build the skill set I would later rely on to manage the business on my own.

As your business grows, you'll have the opportunity to bring in help but early on, keep things lean. Don't assume you need a team of ten to make an impact. Start with what you have and be strategic. When it is time to hire, make sure every person you bring in adds real value not just overhead.

The Fourth Real Hurdle: Marketing

It's Not About Ads - It's About Trust: Rethinking Marketing for Healthcare Entrepreneurs

This part intimidated me the most when I first started.

I thought marketing meant running polished ads, printing glossy brochures, and posting constantly on Facebook and Instagram. So, I did what I thought I was supposed to do. I spent money.

Looking back, I now realize I spent *too much* money on printed ads that didn't give me a strong return. I also tried to engage on social media, but I quickly learned that just being *present* online doesn't guarantee results, especially if you haven't yet built a following or a trusted brand voice.

For someone who was just starting out, with a limited budget and wearing every hat in my business, I needed a different approach.

So, I shifted gears. I simplified. I focused on what I could control.

I started with business cards, printed plaques that clearly outlined my services, and simple flyers that I could leave in the hands of people who would immediately benefit from my services. People like referral sources, home health and hospice agencies, assisted living communities and personal care home, caregivers, families, and community partners. These materials were affordable, clear, and personal. They allowed me to build visibility in a way that matched my bandwidth and resources.

And what I discovered was this: word of mouth is powerful.

In healthcare, when you show up consistently and do meaningful, quality work people talk. Families refer you. Patients remember you. Communities embrace you.

Yes, there's a place for digital marketing, branding, and social media. Those tools can be incredibly valuable when you're ready. But don't let them overwhelm you and definitely don't let them delay your launch. Your reputation is often your strongest campaign.

Marketing in healthcare entrepreneurship isn't about slick slogans or viral content, it's about building trust, showing up for your patients, and creating impact one person at a time.

The Truth About Hurdles

Every entrepreneur faces them.
The difference is how we respond.

Confidence, funding, people, and marketing may seem like barriers, but they're really invitations. Invitations to grow. To learn. To lean into your mission and trust your resourcefulness.

Here's the mindset shift I want you to carry forward:

You are not stuck.
You are not underqualified.
You are not too late.
You are already equipped.

And when the next hurdle comes, and it will, you'll remember that you've faced them before and moved anyway.

Welcome to the shift.

Chapter 4

The One Thing That Will Make or Break Your Business Success

If there's one thing that will keep you grounded through every high and low of entrepreneurship, it's this:

You must be clear on your why.

Not just why the system is broken.
Not just why patients need something different.
But why *you* are the one to bring this vision to life.

When your mission is bigger than your fear, you'll move. When your "why" is real, you won't quit, no matter how hard it gets.

But here's the secret:
Your why is only powerful if you pair it with preparation.

As a healthcare provider stepping into business, you can't just have the heart, you need the strategy. You need to understand not just what you're building, but how to build it.

As nurses and healthcare professionals, our training rarely includes exposure to business, business planning, or entrepreneurship. Understandably, the primary focus is on clinical skills and patient care. Even as advanced practice providers, we seldom receive education on crucial aspects like billing, coding, and how revenue is generated in healthcare. It's no surprise, then, that these areas often become the most intimidating challenges for healthcare professionals.

So, to successfully move from purpose to practice, focusing on these three essentials is crucial

- *Learn the Business of Healthcare*
- *Know Your Resources*
- *Get Business Training*

Learn the Business of Healthcare

It's one thing to have a vision, it's another entirely to build a business that can sustain and support it. Healthcare entrepreneurship isn't fueled by passion alone; it demands a solid understanding of the practical, financial, and operational realities that keep a business running smoothly and sustainably.

Early on, I quickly realized that knowing how to care for patients was only part of the equation. To keep my practice afloat and growing, I had to immerse myself in the nuts and bolts of the business side: billing, insurance credentialing, documentation, coding, and most importantly, deciding which revenue streams best fit my business model. Would I focus on private pay, where patients pay out-of-pocket, or insurance reimbursement, where services are billed to insurance companies? I chose to concentrate on insurance reimbursement because I never wanted a patient to forgo essential care simply because they couldn't afford upfront costs.

That decision meant I needed to significantly enhance my understanding of insurance billing and coding to ensure that I set up my business the right way from the start. This was not something I had been taught during my clinical training. So, I embarked on a journey of self-teaching, drawing heavily from my previous experience in senior leadership roles within home health care. I delved deep into Medicare billing specifics for home-based primary care visits, a complex area with its own unique rules and regulations.

A crucial part of this process involved learning about Current Procedural Terminology (CPT) codes, the standardized codes used to describe medical, surgical, and diagnostic services. These codes serve as the universal language providers use to bill insurance companies and government payers such as Medicare (American Medical Association [AMA], n.d.). Understanding which CPT codes are billable, how to use them correctly, and how they relate to different services was essential. This coding system directly affects how much a healthcare practice is reimbursed, so mistakes can be costly or delay payments.

In addition to CPT codes, I had to learn the subtle but critical differences between fee-for-service and value-based care models. Fee-for-service reimburses providers for each service performed often incentivizing volume over value.

Value-based care ties reimbursement to patient outcomes and cost efficiency, encouraging high-quality, coordinated care (Centers for Medicare & Medicaid Services, n.d.; Chernew, 2011). Understanding how these payment models impact cash flow and practice sustainability was vital for strategic planning.

At first, all of this felt overwhelming especially since I couldn't afford to outsource these tasks. Many entrepreneurs face this same challenge when starting out. But I knew that if I didn't develop at least a working knowledge of these financial and operational mechanics, I would quickly become discouraged and risk failure. So, I pushed through and took things one step at a time, one course at a time. I often used the time between patient visits while I was driving to listen to courses online.

You don't need to master every detail overnight, but you do need to gain enough understanding to confidently navigate your business's financial health. Without that clarity, even the most passionate vision can unravel under the weight of unexpected expenses, delayed reimbursements, or administrative pitfalls.

Remember: you're not building a hobby; you're building a business. That means taking ownership of both your clinical expertise *and* the behind-the-scenes business strategies that will keep your mission alive and thriving for years to come.

Know Your Resources

One of the most important questions you can ask yourself as a new entrepreneur is:

What do I already have?

Resources are the foundation of your entrepreneurial journey and that doesn't just mean money. In fact, many of the most valuable resources you possess may already be right in front of you, waiting to be recognized and leveraged.

People are resources.
Space is a resource.
Time is a resource.
Your energy, skills, experience, and relationships, all of it matters.

When you're just getting started, take time to make a clear and honest inventory of your assets. Think beyond financial capital. What knowledge, networks, and tools do you already have access to? What professional relationships can you lean into? What equipment, office space or technology do you already own?

Start by asking yourself:

- **Am I launching this solo or with a partner?**
  This determines how decisions are made and how responsibilities are shared. A solo launch often means wearing every hat; clinician, marketer, biller, and receptionist, until you can afford to delegate.

- **Can I outsource anything right away, or will I need to manage it all initially?**
  If you're tech-savvy, you might be able to build your own website or handle social media. If not, perhaps a student intern or freelancer can help at a lower cost.

- **Who is my ideal patient or client?**
  Where do they live? What barriers to care are they facing? What problems do they need solved, and how can your service provide relief or convenience?
- **How will they pay?**
  Are they covered by Medicare, Medicaid, private insurance or are they primarily cash pay clients? Knowing this early will influence your billing strategy, credentialing decisions, and marketing approach.

And yes, money matters too. But it's not just about how much you have; it's about how you plan to use it.

- How much startup capital do I truly have access to?
  Are you bootstrapping with personal savings, taking out a small business loan, applying for grants, or seeking investor backing? Each option comes with different expectations, obligations, and timelines.

In my own journey, I launched my practice on a lean budget, making intentional and strategic decisions. I didn't hire a full team right away. Instead, I maximized affordable co-working spaces, tapped into small local business support programs, and leveraged my professional network. I asked for help when I needed it, bartered services, and learned to stretch every dollar.

The fewer assumptions you make, the smarter you can be with your resources. Don't spend money where you don't need to, and don't overlook assets that are already within reach. A laptop and a reliable Wi-Fi connection can be the beginning of a fully operational practice in today's digital world.

Here's the truth: you don't need everything to get started. But you do need to clearly understand what you have, what's missing, and how to fill the gaps strategically. Clarity allows you to make thoughtful decisions, avoid burnout, and focus on building something sustainable from the start.

Get Business Training

You've spent years learning how to care for others. Now it's time to invest just as intentionally in learning how to care for your business.

Business education is not optional. It's the foundation you need to build a strong, sustainable practice. Without it, even the best clinical skills can fall short in an entrepreneurial setting.

But here's the catch: no one's going to hand it to you. Business training doesn't come packaged with your nursing degree or provider license. You have to go out and get it.

I attended conferences.
I joined professional organizations that offered resources and training.
I asked uncomfortable questions.
I sat in rooms where I didn't always feel like I belonged until I realized I did.

At first, it was intimidating. I was no stranger to conversations about revenue targets, profit margins, KPIs, and scaling from my time in clinical operations as a Home Health Director but learning these concepts as a business owner was an entirely different challenge. Still, the more I showed up, the more I grew. You have to intentionally seek out the spaces where business conversations are happening and if they don't exist in your circle, create them.

Expand your circle and your comfort zone.

Growth rarely happens in isolation. It happens when you intentionally step outside of your clinical and professional echo chamber and into rooms where ideas are exchanged freely, feedback is honest, and strategy is the language of the moment.

The Power of Networking

One of the most underrated forms of business training is simply being around other people who are doing what you want to do or have done it before. Networking isn't just a buzzword; it's a survival skill for entrepreneurs.

Don't limit yourself to only healthcare spaces. Yes, it's important to network within healthcare associations, nursing collaboratives, and clinical communities, but true innovation often happens at the intersection of industries. That's why I also sought out:

- Local chambers of commerce
- Minority business associations
- Women's entrepreneurial groups
- Small business development centers
- Start-up incubators and pitch events
- Online business accelerators and mastermind groups

Each of these connections taught me something about funding, marketing, branding, legal compliance, and leadership. And in return, I brought something to the table too: a healthcare perspective grounded in purpose and service.

Be Strategic About Where You Show Up

Not every room will be the right room, but every room offers a lesson. Some teach you skills. Others show you what doesn't work. Either way, you grow.

- Take a course in healthcare finance or medical billing even if it's online.
- Sign up for a business bootcamp that focuses on entrepreneurship fundamentals.
- Subscribe to healthcare business podcasts or newsletters.
- Connect with providers turned entrepreneurs on social media platforms.

The more you surround yourself with people who are *building*, the more you'll stretch your mindset and sharpen your focus.

Remember:

You're not just running a practice, you're running a business. And that requires a different kind of discipline, one built on systems, structure, and strategy.

So yes, get business training. But also build business relationships. Because access to information is powerful, but access to people that's transformational.

But here's **the catch**:
None of it works without intention.

And more importantly, **none of it works without clarity on your "why."**

Your *why* is your anchor.
It's what holds you steady when things get hard (and they will). It's what reminds you that your work matters, on the days when the numbers don't add up and the to-do list feels endless.

Your *why* is what will keep you grounded, focused, and determined, especially when things don't go as planned. Like when that account that once promised to make you their provider of choice suddenly chooses someone else. Or when the same mouth that once sang your praises now speaks against you.

In those moments, your *why* becomes your anchor. It reminds you who you are, why you started, and who you're really doing this for.

So, before we go any deeper, pause and ask yourself:

Why do I want to build this?
Who am I trying to serve?
What does success look like to me?

Get specific. Get honest. Because your "why" will do more than inspire you, it will *guide every business decision you make.*

Your Why Needs a Foundation

A clear why is what gets you moving.
But learning, resourcing, and training is what keeps you going.

This chapter is your invitation to step into the role of entrepreneur, not just emotionally, but practically. Because the dream is only the beginning. You now hold the key to something bigger if you're willing to do the work behind the scenes.

Remember:

You're not just launching a service.
You're building a solution.
You're not just helping people.
You're building something that can *last*.

And that starts by getting clear, not only on *why* you're doing this, but on *how* you'll make it happen.

Chapter 5

The Foundation - Building Your Business Plan with Your "Why" at the Center

By now, you've probably realized that entrepreneurship, especially in healthcare, isn't about finding a magic formula. It's about building something real, rooted in passion, and sustained by strategy.

Now that you've identified your *why*, the deep reason behind why you're pursuing this dream, business, or next step, it's time to build your plan.

But here's the key: **don't overcomplicate it.**
The truth is, too many people get stuck trying to design the "perfect" plan and never start at all. What really matters is

starting simple. The best plans are clear, actionable, and easy to follow. As you grow, your plan will naturally evolve but you'll never gain momentum if you don't take that very first step.

Your *why* is your anchor, and your plan is the map. Together, they give you clarity, focus, and the courage to keep going when challenges come up.

That's where my **Why Worksheet** comes in, it's designed to help you connect your motivation to simple, doable action steps. You can grab your free copy at NursesMindYourBusiness.com

Start with a Plan - But Keep It Simple

You don't need a 40-page investor grade business plan to get started. What you need is a living document; a simple, focused outline that helps you think clearly and make smart decisions as you grow. A business plan is simply a plan for your business. Don't overcomplicate it and realize it is a fluid document.

Here's what that can include:

1. Mission & Vision
- What problems are you solving?
- Who are you solving it for?
- Why does this matter to you?

2. Services Offered
- What exactly are you providing?
- Will this be insurance-based, private pay, or hybrid?
- Will you offer visits in-person, virtual, or both?

3. Target Audience
- Who is your ideal patient or client?

- What's their age, location, insurance coverage, and biggest challenge?
- Where do they currently get care or fall through the cracks?

4. Pricing Model
- How will you charge?
- Will you bill insurance? If so, which ones?
- What does your pricing need to be to stay sustainable?

5. Marketing Strategy
- How will people find you?
- Will your marketing be word-of-mouth, digital, community-based?
- How will you track what's working?

6. Milestones
- What goals can you set to track progress?
- How many clients do you want before reducing hours at your current job?
- What financial benchmarks will you use?

These questions help you root your business in purpose, not just process. They guide your priorities and give your work meaning on the hard days.

For me, my mission was crystal clear:
"Providing Home-Based Primary Care, Wherever You Call Home."

That mission statement didn't just sit on a website. It fueled every decision I made from the services I offered to the partnerships I pursued. It kept me focused on a population I cared deeply about and helped me develop a practice tailored to their specific needs.

Your mission is your compass. Your vision is the future you're working toward. Together, they form the foundation of your business and ensure that growth doesn't lead you away from what matters most.

In Summary: Let Your Plan Be a Guide, Not a Barrier

Your business plan doesn't have to be complicated; it just has to be clear. This is not about impressing investors; it's about giving yourself a roadmap. When you define your mission, clarify your services, identify your audience, and outline a basic pricing and marketing strategy, you're giving structure to your vision.

Think of this plan as your foundation. It's flexible, not fixed. It will grow and evolve as you do but starting with even a simple version helps you move forward with purpose and direction.

So don't wait until everything is perfect. Begin with what you know and build as you go. Let your mission lead the way, your plan supports your steps, and your passion keeps you grounded. Every great business starts with clarity, not complexity.

Managing Expectations: Don't Quit Your Day Job (Yet)

This is the part many people skip because it's not flashy. But it's necessary.

When I launched my business, I didn't walk away from everything and jump in with both feet. I had a full-time job. Then I transitioned to four PRN jobs, slowly tapering off as my patient load increased.

I set goals- specific, measurable targets that represented progress. They gave me something to work toward and helped me make smart decisions rooted in reality, not emotion. I told myself, *"Once I reach 25 patients, I can let go of one job."* That became my benchmark, and I stayed true to it.

Eventually, I reached that threshold. Then another. I was able to walk away from all PRN work and operate my practice full time.

But even then, I didn't pay myself right away.

It took three full years before I consistently wrote myself a paycheck.

And I want to say that out loud, because far too many nurse entrepreneurs feel like something is wrong with them when they don't hit profit immediately. But this is the truth: it's normal. It's just not always talked about.

From day one, I prioritized paying my employees and covering every operational cost with integrity and consistency. That mattered more to me than drawing a salary. I knew that the trust of my team and the strength of my infrastructure would determine whether this business was sustainable in the long run.

Entrepreneurship takes time.
Growth takes time.

Your income might look different in the beginning and that's okay.

Don't let someone else's highlight reel rush your process. There's no shame in building in stages. In fact, it's a sign of wisdom.

So, while you're building:

- Keep your financial responsibilities covered.
- Create safety nets.
- Give yourself grace.

You might be the last person to get paid. You might have to hustle longer than you thought. But what you're doing is planting seeds for something that lasts, not just profitable, but purposeful.

This isn't about "arriving."
It's about building something worth arriving to.

MIND YOUR BUSINESS TRUTH #3

Success Isn't Instant - But It Is Possible

This is not an overnight success story. And I'm not here to sell you one.

What I can promise is this: if you commit to your mission, stay grounded in your why, and build with intention, your business will grow. It will be sustainable, meaningful, and impactful.

But it has to be rooted in reality, not just hope.

So, build smart. Start simple. Stay focused.

The Model - Where Passion Meets Process and Connects your "Why"

You've done the deep work. You've clarified your why, confronted the hurdles that hold most people back, and outlined the early pieces of your business plan. You've laid the foundation now it's time to build the structure.

This next phase of your journey is all about *execution*.

The Model is where we break it all down, step by step. This is the part where your idea begins to take shape in the real world. It's where you learn how to:

- Set up your business structure
- Choose the right model for your goals
- Get paid legally and sustainably
- Find and serve your first clients
- Establish systems that grow with you

In other words: this is where you move from *concept* to *company*.

Let's be clear, you don't have to do it all at once. But you *do* have to take the next step. Because an idea, no matter how powerful, doesn't build itself. You build it with the right knowledge, the right strategy, and the right mindset.

This is the part most healthcare providers never get exposed to. We've been trained to deliver care, follow protocols, and rely on institutions for structure. But in entrepreneurship, *you* are the structure.

You are responsible for setting the expectations and the culture of your organization.

And that's a beautiful thing because it means you get to build something that truly reflects your values, your voice, and your vision.

You don't need perfection.
You don't need permission.
You need movement and a framework to support it.

So, let's take everything you've clarified so far and begin to shape it into a business that serves, sustains, and scales.

Chapter 6

The Core Mechanism: Choosing Your Business Model

At the heart of every sustainable business is a **core mechanism**, a system, a strategy, a structure that keeps everything running. But for me, the engine that powered every decision I made wasn't built on spreadsheets or software.

It was built on people.

"People first" is the principle that drove everything I did and still do.
Not profits first.
Not convenience first.
People. First.

When I saw individuals who were homebound, trapped in a system that didn't make space for them, I knew I couldn't just keep showing up the same way. These weren't just patients.

They were grandmothers, veterans, neighbors, and parents. People who deserved care that came to *them* when they could no longer come to us.

That realization became the foundation of my business model.

"People first. It is my core principle in business and in life. I just believe that if you put people first and lead with compassion that everything else falls into place" (commencement address, South University, June 2024)

Your Business Model Starts With Your Mission

A lot of people choose their business model based on trends or revenue projections. And while those things matter, they don't create longevity. What does? A model that aligns with your mission.

For me, that meant never losing the clinical side of my identity. I love leadership, but I never wanted to leave patient care behind.

In fact, during my time in home health care, I initially turned down the clinical manager position, a role that didn't align with how I saw myself professionally at the time, but ultimately helped shape the leader I would become. I wasn't interested in a role that pulled me too far from my patients. But then I had a thought: *What if I could define the role instead of letting the role define me?*

So, I did.

I kept seeing patients. I led the team, sat through meetings, ran reports and headed out to provide patient care. And yes,

I had moments where I felt like I was reenacting that scene from a comic superhero, changing from business attire into scrubs in my office so I could do both. It often meant I was working longer hours to keep up with the demands of overseeing the responsibilities of clinical management. But it mattered to me. Staying connected to patient care *grounded* me. It kept me aligned with my purpose.

Later, when I was promoted to director and area director, I carried the same mindset with me. I didn't climb the clinical ladder to escape patient care, I used my position to *stay rooted in it*, while expanding my reach.

After years of working in home healthcare as a Registered Nurse, I began to feel the limits of my role. I could assess patients, identify their problems, and communicate with families but I couldn't implement the solutions I knew they needed. I would see a patient struggling without essential medical equipment, but I couldn't order it. I'd recognize clear signs that a patient needed physical or occupational therapy, but I had to wait on someone else to make the referral.

Eventually, I made the decision to go back to school and become a Nurse Practitioner. Why? Because I saw repeatedly the difference a Nurse Practitioner could make, not just in diagnosing, but in *acting*. I also realized that it was the key to more; more knowledge, more clinical skill, more autonomy, more impact and, most importantly-more people to serve.

That growing awareness became the driving force behind my next step. I didn't want to just recognize problems anymore, I wanted to be the one who could solve them.

Becoming a Nurse Practitioner gave me the tools to do exactly that. It expanded my reach and allowed me to serve a larger, often forgotten population: the homebound, the elderly, and those with limited access to care. It gave me a seat at the table and a voice in decisions that truly affected patient outcomes.

I didn't pursue this path just for the title or the credentials. I did it because I saw firsthand that being able to act on what I knew could mean the difference between decline and recovery, between isolation and dignity, between suffering and quality of life for so many patients.

And now, with that knowledge, I could do something more than care, I could lead, change, and heal.

When the Model You Need Doesn't Exist, Build It

I remember explaining my plan to a colleague with so much excitement. *I said, "I want to create a way to serve patients in their homes."* We discussed my years of experience and how the very people I've spent years advocating for would be the foundation of my business. We even talked about the need being there, and how the model doesn't exist yet. I eagerly added, *"So if I can't find it, I'll build it."*

But instead of encouragement or open doors, the response was silence. Crickets.

That moment taught me something important: **just because the need is obvious to you, doesn't mean the world is ready to hand you the solution.** That's when I realized the power of having a strong *why*, because when the doors don't open easily, your *why* is what keeps you knocking, creating, and moving forward.

There were no doors opening. No invitations. No enthusiasm. Just silence.

I went door to door, meeting with various healthcare organizations, presenting home-based primary care as a **viable, strategic solution** to meet the growing needs of our community. I highlighted the gaps in access, identified patients at high risk for rehospitalization, and offered partnership opportunities that could improve outcomes while reducing strain on the system.

Still, the idea wasn't immediately embraced. It would have been easy to walk away but I knew what I saw was real. So, I kept going. I embraced the silence as a challenge and turned it into momentum.

I built my own box.

I started my own home-based primary care practice not because I had always dreamed of being an entrepreneur, but because I could no longer compromise the kind of care I knew people deserved. I wasn't chasing a business, I was answering a calling.

At the time, there were no other agencies like mine in the community I lived in. Despite a growing, underserved population of older adults who clearly needed accessible care, no one was doing it. No one had created the model. So, I did.

By then, I had over 15 years of experience in home healthcare, working in roles that ranged from registered nurse (RN) in the field to clinical director, and eventually area director overseeing multiple operations across Southeast Georgia. I had seen the gaps up close, the patients who couldn't leave their homes, the families struggling to coordinate care, the providers stretched thin and unable to reach those most in need.

I brought the idea to the table over and over again: *Why not bring the provider to the patient? Why not meet people where they are?*

And every time, I was met with the same response: silence.

It would've been easy to walk away. To accept the status quo. To believe that if it wasn't already being done, maybe it couldn't be done.

But instead, I made a choice:
I stopped waiting for someone else to lead.
I stopped asking for permission.
I embraced change, leaned into the uncertainty, and redefined the path forward.

I took everything I had learned from leadership, clinical practice, and healthcare operations, and used it to build a patient-centered, mission-driven model, one rooted in dignity, access, and trust.

I say this not to glorify the struggle, but to remind you:
If the model you need doesn't exist, you can build it.
You don't have to fit into someone else's box.
You can design your own.

Life is filled with unexpected turns. Some of the most meaningful breakthroughs happen when we step outside of our comfort zones. Embrace the challenges, they are not setbacks, they are stepping stones. Let failure refine you, not define you.

And don't allow others to write your narrative. Define yourself.

You get to choose the path that aligns with your purpose. You get to lead the way.

Because sometimes, the silence you hear isn't rejection, it's a signal. A signal that *you* were meant to go first.

And that's the secret: your business model is your vehicle, but your mission is the fuel.

When Defining Your Model: Start With These Questions

You don't need to follow someone else's blueprint. You need to create a model that reflects *you*. Ask yourself:

- Do I want to work solo, or build a team?
- Do I want to go mobile, stay virtual, or open a physical location?
- Will I accept insurance, offer private pay, or create a hybrid?
- What population do I want to serve and how do they access care now?
- What services am I passionate about providing and which ones can I delegate?

For me, the model that made sense was a **mobile, solo practice** focused on home-based primary care for older adults. I kept my overhead low, stayed lean, and stayed close to the patient.

That alignment between my model and my mission is what made the business sustainable.

Your Model Must Serve Your Mission

Never forget: **your business should serve your mission - not the other way around.**

It's easy to get lost in the logistics: LLCs vs. S-Corps, private pay vs. billing, overhead vs. outsourcing. Those are important decisions but they're *second* to your purpose.

What gave my business life wasn't a perfect plan. It was a relentless focus on *who* I was here to serve and *why* they needed me to show up differently.

So, as you shape your model, let it reflect:

- What you believe in
- What you're committed to
- And who you refuse to leave behind

Because when you get clear on that, the rest starts to fall into place.

Chapter 7

Creating Your Business: Legal, Licensing & Logistics

Every entrepreneurial journey has a starting point, a natural path that calls to you. For me, that path was home-based primary care, shaped by my years of experience in home healthcare. For you, it might be something different. The key is to listen to *your instinct*, do your research, and trust that your business will find you.

Start With Your Natural Path

The best advice I can give is: **Follow what feels right for you.**

Don't try to force a model that doesn't fit your passion or your skillset. If home-based primary care speaks to you, explore it. If telehealth, wellness coaching, or something else calls your name, dive in. There's no one-size-fits-all path in entrepreneurship, especially in healthcare. Your lived experiences, your strengths, and your values are what make your business unique. Let them guide you.

And remember, less is best, especially in the beginning. As I mentioned before, start with the resources you already have and be intentional in how you build your business. Equally, protect your vision as carefully as you develop it, and be selective about when and with whom you share it.

When you're just starting out, it's often wise to keep your business idea close to the chest. Not because people are out to steal it, but because unsolicited opinions, even from well-meaning friends and colleagues, can unintentionally chip away at your confidence. They can cause you to second-guess your instincts or stall your momentum before you've even begun.

Your idea doesn't need validation from everyone. It just needs you to protect it long enough to bring it to life.

That protection isn't just emotional, it's strategic too. Especially if you're developing proprietary content, a unique model of care, or a niche offering that isn't widely available. Be mindful about how much you share, when you share, and with whom. **Your intellectual property is valuable, and it deserves protection.**

Don't underestimate the power of a simple, standardized Non-Disclosure Agreement (NDA). If you're entering conversations that involve your business model, training material, or strategy, even with peers or potential collaborators, come prepared with an NDA. It's not just about legal coverage. It's about sending a clear message: **your work is intentional, professional, and worth safeguarding.**

I'll be honest, I had to learn this the hard way.

I've always been someone who shares freely. I'm passionate about my work, and when people ask for advice, I offer it. That part of me hasn't changed.

But over time, I realized just how valuable those conversations were. The questions kept coming. The guidance I was giving off the cuff, from the heart, was solving real problems for people. It was helping them move forward, just like I had.

That's when I shifted.

I began to be more intentional. I launched a consulting business, not just to formalize the support I was already providing, but to create a **sustainable, structured way** to help others on their journey without depleting myself in the process.

Sharing your knowledge isn't the problem. But doing it without boundaries or strategy can hold you back.

You don't have to shrink to protect your vision, but you do need to steward it wisely. Build in silence when you need to. Move with purpose. And when you're ready, let your results speak louder than your plans ever could.

Be Loud Where It Counts

That said, don't isolate yourself. While it's wise to protect your idea in its early stages, it's just as important to put yourself in the right rooms, especially those that stretch you beyond your comfort zone.

Instead of sharing your plans casually at the water cooler or among people who may not understand your vision, be intentional about where and how you show up. Attend conferences. Join networking events. Get in rooms where the conversations are different, where business, growth, and innovation are the focus.

As nurses, we're not always taught to think in business terms. But we must. That means joining business organizations, attending entrepreneurial meetups and stepping into spaces where you're surrounded by people who think like owners and decision-makers. It may feel unfamiliar at first, but that's where the growth happens.

These spaces are golden. You're likely rubbing shoulders with future business partners, investors, collaborators, and stakeholders even if you don't realize it yet. A single conversation could lead to a contract. A coffee meeting could turn into mentorship. The connection you make today might become the partnership that changes everything tomorrow.

I once met a fellow healthcare professional at a small community networking breakfast. We started chatting over coffee about the challenges of providing care in assisted living communities. Two weeks later, she called to invite me to speak at an open house for the assisted living community she managed, an opportunity that not only showcased my expertise but also connected me with new referral sources and potential clients.

And beyond opportunity, this kind of networking builds confidence. It reinforces that you belong in these spaces. It reminds you that you are not alone and that there's an entire world of professionals who are rooting for your success and eager to collaborate.

So be bold. Be strategic. Be loud where it counts. Because your next breakthrough might just be one introduction away.

A Real-Time Example: How I Created My Business

When I first started, I typed *"house calls as a business model"* into a search bar; just curious where it might lead. That simple search opened the door to a network of advanced practice providers already living the vision I had in my heart. I followed their programs, studied their approaches, and learned from their successes and challenges. It also introduced me to national organizations devoted to advancing home-based primary care. I didn't just join; I jumped in with both feet. I attended their conferences, volunteered for their planning committees, and surrounded myself with people who spoke the language of my future. I became a student again, asking questions, taking notes, and soaking in every ounce of wisdom. Each connection, each conversation, was a steppingstone toward building the practice I had once only imagined

You don't have to reinvent the wheel. Learn from those who have walked the path.

Here's a simplified list of steps I followed to get my business off the ground:

- Select a business name that reflects your brand, mission, and values, while being easy to remember and legally available. (Fun fact: My children named my business!)
- Register your business in your state.

- Consider your structure: S-Corp vs LLC vs. DBA.
- Get your Employer Identification Number (EIN) from the IRS.
- Use a professional business address, such as a co-working space instead of your home address.
  - » **Tip:** Begin with the end in mind. Consider that once your business information is published online, it can be difficult to change or remove. Protect your privacy from the start by avoiding the use of your home address
- Open a dedicated business bank account. This is crucial for separating your personal and business finances, and you'll need your EIN and LLC documents for this.
- Use "we" and "us" in your communications. Perception matters. Whether it's on your website, social media, business cards, or marketing materials, present yourself as a company rather than just an individual. Even if you're a solo operation, speak from the perspective of your brand. The brand might be your service or even you personally but refer to it as the business, not just yourself. This helps convey stability, credibility, and the capacity to serve clients professionally.

Tip: Depending on where you are in hiring and building your team, you will need to understand basic human resources (HR) tasks, such as creating offer letters, completing I-9 verification, or outsourcing certain HR responsibilities. Knowing these fundamentals early on will help you build a strong, compliant team and avoid unnecessary headaches down the road.

Know Your Legal and Licensing Requirements

Before you can serve patients, you must understand and meet the legal and licensing requirements that govern your practice. This isn't just paperwork, it's the foundation that protects your patients, your license, and your business. One of the first lessons I learned when starting my practice was just how important it is to know these requirements inside and out.

The following considerations are essential as you navigate your legal and licensing requirements to stay compliant and prepared:

- What does your county or state require for licensing your business?
- Depending on the state, Advanced Practice Registered Nurses (APRNs), such as Nurse Practitioners, may be required to maintain a collaborative agreement with a physician to provide patient care.
- What laws govern your scope of practice? Are your professional certification and clinical credentialing up to date?
- Are there federal requirements relevant to your services? For example, are you prescribing medications, performing certain procedures, or providing wellness oversight? Depending on the services you offer, there are critical compliance requirements that must be met.
- Organize all your business documents, licensing, and credentialing information in one easily accessible place right from the start. This includes essential paperwork like licenses, certifications, contracts, and insurance

details. For us as nurses and clinicians, that also means keeping track of your registered nurse (RN) license number, advanced practice certification number, U.S. Drug Enforcement Administration (DEA) registration, and Provider Enrollment, Chain, and Ownership System (PECOS) enrollment information. You'll find yourself needing to reference the same documents often. In my case, because I was mobile and frequently seeing patients while managing the business, I created an electronic "operational manual" to store and organize everything. It kept me efficient, compliant, and always prepared.

- If you plan to accept insurance, you'll need to set up accounts with CAQH ProView and Availity:
  - » **CAQH** stands for the **Council for Affordable Quality Healthcare.** Their ProView platform is where you upload and manage your professional credentials such as your state license, DEA, board certification, malpractice insurance, and more. Insurance payers use this information to verify your credentials and complete the credentialing process (Council for Affordable Quality Healthcare, n.d.).
  - » **Availity** is a web-based clearinghouse that connects providers with insurance companies. It allows you to check patient eligibility, submit insurance claims, track reimbursements, and handle other billing-related communications (Practice Solutions, 2022)

Tip: Keep your CAQH profile updated and "attested" every 120 days to avoid delays. Once credentialed, link your payers

CREATING YOUR BUSINESS: LEGAL, LICENSING & LOGISTICS

through Availty to streamline your billing workflow and avoid payment issues.

- Credentialing is another critical step, and it pays to start strategically. Credentialing is the gateway to getting paid so it's essential to get it right early in your business journey.
  » **Credentialing** is the process by which healthcare providers' qualifications, experience, and professional background are verified by insurance companies or healthcare organizations. This process ensures that providers meet established standards to deliver care and be reimbursed for services (Patel & Sharma, 2025).
  » **Insurance credentialing** specifically involves verifying a provider's eligibility to join an insurance network and bill the insurer for services rendered.
  » **Provider credentialing** generally refers to the broader verification of licenses, certifications, education, work history, and malpractice history before granting privileges at a healthcare facility or participation in payer networks. (National Committee for Quality Assurance [NCQA], n.d.)

Credentialing directly impacts how and when you'll be reimbursed, making it one of the most critical operational steps to address up front. Before deciding which insurance companies to create credentials with, take time to research your region and identify which insurers are most prominent in your area. Prioritizing the right payers ensures that your efforts align with the coverage your patient population is most likely to have saving you time, money, and administrative headaches down the line.

» It's also important to note that credentialing often comes with costs, both in time and money. In the beginning, I couldn't afford to hire a credentialing specialist, so I did it myself. Let me tell you; it was *very* cumbersome. I started with Medicare, since it represented the largest portion of my target patient population. It was not an easy process; the application was tedious and time-consuming. After that, I moved on to Medicaid and eventually transitioned to Medicare Advantage and replacement plans.

» Over time, as my business grew and my resources expanded, I was able to outsource credentialing to a professional company and it was a game-changer.

» Credentialing matters, especially when it comes to billing insurance. Many secondary insurers require documented proof of licensure, certification, and enrollment in systems like PECOS. Thanks to my experience as a home healthcare Area Director and in clinical operations, I was already familiar with payer systems and knew how to identify which insurances were most widely used in my county. That knowledge helped me build a sustainable foundation from the start.

With credentialing in place, the next critical step is securing your National Provider Identifier (NPI), which formally recognizes you as an independent provider in the healthcare system. Applying for a National Provider Identifier (NPI) is a unique step for those entering healthcare practice as independent providers. It's essential for billing and insurance. An NPI, or National Provider Identifier, is a unique 10-digit identification number issued by the Centers for Medicare & Medicaid Services (CMS) to healthcare providers in the United States. It is required for any provider who transmits health information electronically for billing or administrative purposes. There are two types of NPIs: Type 1 for individual providers and Type 2 for organizations or group practices (Centers for Medicare & Medicaid Services, n.d.).

Type 1 NPI- Individual Providers

You need an Individual Provider (Type 1) NPI if you are any of the following:

- **Nurse Practitioners (APRNs)**
- **Physicians**
- **Physician Assistants**
- **Registered Nurses (if billing for services)**
- **Therapists** (e.g., physical, occupational, speech)
- **Dentists**
- **Clinical Social Workers**

If you plan to bill insurance (including Medicare/Medicaid) as yourself (either independently or as part of a group), you must have a Type 1 NPI.

Type 2 NPI – Organizations or Group Practices

You need an Organizational Provider (Type 2) NPI if you are any of the following:

- Primary care clinics
- Group practices
- Home health agencies
- Behavioral health practices
- Any healthcare business that operates as an LLC, corporation, or other legal entity

If you've formed a business entity to bill insurance, you'll need a Type 2 NPI in addition to your personal Type 1 NPI.

Chapter 8

Preparing to See Clients: Where Preparation Meets Purpose

Once your business is legally and logistically sound, it's time to see patients, take on your first client, engage with your potential referral sources, and begin building lasting relationships that will grow your practice.

This is where preparation meets purpose.

What equipment and supplies do you need?
For me that meant that I had to carefully assemble my gear to ensure I could deliver high-quality care on the road. When you're operating outside of a traditional clinical setting, your equipment becomes your mobile toolkit. Every item should be intentional, reliable, and easy to transport.

I invested in a durable, well-organized medical bag. Inside, I packed essentials like:

- A blood pressure cuff and stethoscope
- Pulse oximeter and thermometer
- Otoscope and ophthalmoscope
- Basic wound care supplies (bandages, dressings, antiseptics)
- PPE (gloves, masks, hand sanitizer)
- A tablet or laptop with a secure electronic medical record (EMR) system for documenting on the go
- A prescription pad (until I could afford to transition to electronic prescribing)
- HIPAA-compliant forms, consent documents, and a clipboard
- Backup chargers, a mobile hotspot for internet access, and occasional access to a printer or scanner

Depending on my patient population, I also kept extras on hand like incontinence supplies, sterile urine cups, and specimen collection kits.

You don't need to start with everything, but you do need a functional setup that allows you to deliver safe, competent care. Build your supply list based on your services and the needs of your clients. It's better to grow into your gear than to overpack with items you rarely use.

Key Tip: Don't forget the other side of mobile care - diagnostics and referrals.

Whether it's blood work, imaging, or specialist consultations, this is where you begin building your extended healthcare network. You don't have to do everything yourself. In fact, you shouldn't.

You become the orchestrator of care facilitating, coordinating, referring where appropriate and advocating on behalf of the clients you serve.

Delivering healthcare beyond the four walls of a clinic takes planning, intention, and heart. I had to get very clear on what I needed, not just in tools, but in partnerships to bring high-quality care right to my patients' front doors.

I drew heavily on my background as a home health clinician. My setup was simple and familiar: my stethoscope, manual blood pressure cuff, and pulse oximeter formed the foundation of my kit. Over time, I added an otoscope, a portable scale, and of course, personal protective equipment, gloves, masks, barriers, especially critical for infection control and patient safety. I didn't need a high-tech mobile unit or expensive gadgets. I kept it lean, functional, and focused on what mattered most: assessing and treating patients safely and effectively in their own homes.

But beyond the equipment, I knew I couldn't do it all alone. I became intentional about collaborating with community-based resources that could help expand the care I provided.

That meant building bridges with home health agencies, many of which were the same ones I had worked with years before.

In some cases, I found myself reconnecting with colleagues who had once reported to me when I was in leadership roles. Over the years, I hired licensed practical nurses (LPNs), schedulers, intake coordinators, and sales representatives who became trusted professionals and advocates in their own right. These were the very connections that eventually supported my practice, creating a strong network that enhanced patient care and helped my business thrive. It was both humbling and rewarding to come full circle and now partner with these colleagues as a business owner, working together toward a shared mission.

> *Let me pause to emphasize the value of empathy and thoughtfulness in every interaction. I learned firsthand how important it is to always treat people with kindness and compassion. Staying courteous and respectful creates relationships you can return to and be welcomed back into.*
>
> *What I didn't realize at the time was that many of the people I once worked with, and even those who worked for me, would later become the very ones who helped build my business. They not only referred patients to me, but they would also comment on my values, professionalism and work ethic.*
>
> *My advice is simple: lead with kindness, remain objective, and be consistent in how you treat others. These core values don't just shape who you are, they create the kind of long-lasting business relationships that sustain success.*

I also established relationships with durable medical equipment (DME) providers, hospice agencies, mobile diagnostic companies, and mobile phlebotomy services. I essentially partnered with anyone and everyone who could help my patients get the care they needed, at home, on time, and with dignity.

These partnerships didn't just make my job easier, they made my patients' lives better. By collaborating across the continuum, I became an orchestrator of care. My role wasn't to do everything myself, it was to connect the dots, educate patients and families, and build care plans that reflected both medical needs and patient choice.

This approach reinforced the idea that home-based care is not isolated care. It's a coordinated, patient-centered model that honors autonomy while delivering excellence. And it all starts with being prepared: knowing your tools, knowing your resources, and knowing your why.

Growing Your Team on Your Terms - Building a Team with Heart and Purpose

As my practice began to grow, I reached a point where I could no longer do it all on my own and that was a good thing. Bringing on team members was both an exciting milestone and a challenging shift. One of the great benefits of running your own business is flexibility and I leaned into that fully.

I wasn't restricted to a rigid 9-to-5, Monday-through-Friday structure. Instead, I was able to build a team that fit the real lives of the people I hired. If someone could only work Tuesdays and Thursdays, great. If another person was only available on Mondays, I made that work. I didn't just fill roles, I looked for individuals whose values aligned with the mission of the business. I built my team around people, not just positions.

That flexibility allowed me to prioritize mission over mechanics. I wasn't looking for perfection; I was looking for heart. I wanted people who cared about the patients as deeply as I did, and who understood the importance of showing up with compassion, flexibility, and commitment.

But I'll be honest; learning to trust others with my business was a growing pain. After all, I had built this practice from the ground up. Every patient. Every family. Every phone call. I had touched every part of the business personally, and it meant a great deal to me that everyone who came into contact with my practice felt heard, understood, and supported.

Letting go of full control wasn't easy, but it was necessary. I realized that in order to expand the impact of my work, I had to release the idea that only *I* could do it right. I trained my team carefully. I emphasized not just clinical excellence, but empathy, listening, and responsiveness. I wanted every patient and every family to feel like they mattered, because they do.

Building a team isn't just about hiring help. It's about building trust, protecting your mission, and creating a culture that reflects what your business stands for. And when you do it right, it doesn't just free up your time, it multiplies your impact.

Putting It All Together

Creating your business is part art, part science, a unique blend of heart and strategy. You're not just launching a company; you're building something that reflects your passion, your purpose, and your personality. At the same time, you're navigating legal requirements, structuring operations, organizing logistics, and making sure your foundation is solid.

You'll find yourself wearing many hats, visionary, administrator, care provider, marketer, and strategist. Some days you'll feel confident and empowered; other days you'll wonder if you're in over your head. That's normal. The key is to keep moving. One decision at a time. One task at a time. One patient at a time.

The truth is, there is no perfect blueprint. There's no one-size-fits-all approach. Your journey will have twists, learning curves, and moments of doubt. But every step you take, no matter how small, is progress.

Here's what matters most:

- **Trust your path.** You saw a need, and you stepped up to meet it. That makes you a leader and a change agent.
- **Keep your focus.** Don't get distracted by what others are doing. Your mission is unique, and your work matters.
- **Stay organized.** From credentialing documents to clinical protocols, build systems that help you manage the day-to-day so you can focus on what matters, serving people.

And remember you don't have to have it all figured out. Your business will evolve, just like you will. Be open to change. Allow room for growth. Let your patients and your experience teach you what works.

The process might feel overwhelming at times, but this is how great things are built. Step by step. Patient by patient. Decision by decision.

In the end, you're not just creating a business. You're building a movement. One that brings care to the people who need it most, in the way that honors their dignity and your calling.

And that's something truly worth building.

Chapter 9

The Critical Component: Finding and Serving Your First Clients

Starting a business as a healthcare provider isn't just about paperwork or marketing plans, it's about envisioning yourself in the role.

Before I ever answered my first call or knocked on a patient's door, I spent time imagining the entire process. I pictured myself receiving a phone call, driving across town, and providing care directly in someone's home.

I thought deeply about the impact of *not* being there, that if I didn't step up, that patient might go without the care they desperately needed.

This mental rehearsal wasn't just daydreaming, it was preparation.

Because to succeed, you must first see yourself as the solution to your client's problem.

You must believe that *you* are the person who can fill the gap, bridge the distance, and make a difference.

The Power of Vision

Visualizing your role isn't about pretending it's already perfect or effortless. It's about internalizing your mission so fully that it becomes a driving force, guiding your daily actions and decisions. For me, visualization became a powerful tool early on, I would picture the patients who needed my care, imagine the long car rides ahead, and mentally rehearse the assessments I would perform in their homes.

This wasn't just daydreaming; it was intentional preparation. By vividly imagining each step, I was able to prepare myself emotionally and mentally for the work ahead. It helped me anticipate challenges and stay grounded when the reality of the job felt overwhelming.

But visualization extended beyond patient care it became essential in marketing my practice and educating others about the value of home-based primary care. I pictured the conversations I wanted to have with potential referral sources, the questions they might ask, and the way I could clearly communicate the benefits of this care model. I envisioned presentations, networking events, and casual encounters where I could plant seeds of understanding and build support.

This vision fueled my confidence, strengthened my resolve, and became a source of motivation during the inevitable hurdles of starting something new. Whenever doubt crept in or exhaustion weighed me down, returning to that clear mental picture reminded me why I started and gave me the energy to keep going.

Visualization turned my mission into a tangible, lived experience that I carried with me every day.

From Inspiration to Validation

With your foundation in place and your initial steps underway, the next challenge can feel like the biggest:
What's the right business idea for me?

It's a question that's both exciting and overwhelming. You've come this far, you're clear on your "why," you've started mapping out your business, maybe even begun offering services to clients. And yet, the pressure to land on the *perfect* idea can cause hesitation.

Here's the truth:
The right idea rarely shows up fully formed.

Instead, it reveals itself through exploration, trial and error, and by paying close attention to what both you and your community truly need.

In my case, every phone call that came in with a question or a request often became the next service I offered in my business. I learned to listen closely because the needs people shared weren't just gaps in care. They were opportunities to expand my impact and expand my business.

During the height of the COVID-19 pandemic, for example, residents of assisted living communities couldn't leave their homes but they still needed access to primary care. I began receiving calls asking if I would come to these communities to provide services like medication management, chronic disease support, and complex care for those with dementia, cognitive impairment, and anxiety.

My answer was yes. And with that, a new branch of my business was born. It would go on to become one of the most expansive and impactful parts of my practice.

Later, I started getting calls from families and assisted living communities requesting move-in assessments. I live in a region experiencing significant growth, particularly among older adults relocating to the area. Many of these communities require documentation from a primary care provider before a potential resident can move in. Physical assessments, medication reconciliation, and prescriptions sent to a pharmacy are all the elements needed to ensure continuity of care. But here's the problem: these individuals typically hadn't established care with a local primary care provider yet. And with wait times of 6–8 weeks just to get an initial appointment, their move-in dates were at risk.

Once again, I became the solution. I met families and patients exactly where they were, sometimes in parking lots, hotel rooms, or right on-site at the community they would soon call home.

By meeting patients and families exactly where they were, I was able to step in quickly, ensuring continuity of care and establishing relationships that would soon grow into a broader network of referrals.

As my presence grew, so did the calls from hospital case managers, home health agencies, and hospice organizations. These professionals identified patients who lacked a primary care provider but desperately needed one to continue essential care.

Hospital case managers relied on me to bridge the gap for patients transitioning from the hospital back to their homes. In my role supporting transitional care management, I quickly stepped in to follow patients post-discharge, helping reduce their risk of readmission.

I remember one patient in particular who hadn't seen a primary care provider in over 15 years. This patient was hesitant to visit clinics due to past negative experiences and mistrust. Yet, when I offered a visit at home, the patient welcomed the care. Over time, that visit grew into regular support, helping the patient manage chronic conditions and regain confidence in the health journey.

Many of my patients shared similar stories. Individuals who either avoided clinics due to mobility or cognitive challenges or who simply felt disconnected from traditional healthcare. They weren't willing or able to come to a clinic, but they were open to someone coming to them. And that someone was me.

Home health agencies also relied on my practice. In order to initiate or continue care, they needed a provider to oversee the plan of care, sign documentation, and manage treatment. *(Full disclosure: laws vary by state. In Georgia, partway through my business journey, the rules around nurse practitioners certifying and managing home health services changed. As a provider, this was both frustrating and concerning, especially because of how it affects patients' access to care. But that's a whole other conversation, one I'll save for another time.)*

Hospice agencies, too, found support in my services. They often had patients who no longer qualified for hospice care but still required continued support. Without an established primary care provider, these patients faced the risk of having their care disrupted. I became the seamless option to continue their medical management, including medication oversight, helping them transition safely and with dignity.

Each call, each referral, each "Can you help with this?" was another opportunity to grow, not just my business, but the impact I could have. My practice wasn't built overnight. It was built through listening, responding, and showing up again and again for the people who needed care the most.

Each of these scenarios taught me something essential: **the business you build will grow from the problems you're willing to solve.**

All you have to do is listen, respond with intention, and allow your services to evolve based on the real needs of your community.

I encourage you to cut through the noise. You'll learn how to quickly identify and validate business ideas that align with your skills, your passion, and the real-world needs of the people you want to serve.

Because once you begin to truly see yourself as the solution, the leader, the innovator, the provider, clarity starts to rise above the noise. Confidence grows. And when the right idea does find you, you won't hesitate. You'll be ready to build it with boldness and momentum, knowing that you're not just filling a gap, you're answering a call.

MIND YOUR BUSINESS TRUTH #4

Don't Lose Track of Time

Move at the speed of business. Simply put, don't procrastinate and lose valuable time when launching a business.

Time is the one resource you can't get back.

The sooner you begin testing your idea in the real world, the sooner you'll discover what works, what needs adjusting, and what's worth letting go. Every step you take in motion becomes a form of learning, an insight, a refinement, a confirmation.

Waiting too long to start can quietly sabotage your momentum. It leads to missed opportunities, mounting self-doubt, and often burnout. I've seen so many brilliant healthcare professionals sit on powerful ideas out of fear, over-planning, or waiting for "the right time." But the truth is, clarity comes through action.

So don't wait to get perfect. Just start.

In the pages ahead, I'll walk you through a practical, repeatable approach to uncovering the *right* idea for you and your community. You'll learn how to:

- Generate business ideas grounded in your lived experience and passions
- Spot the real problems your future clients are facing
- Test those ideas quickly with minimal risk
- Validate what your market truly needs before investing big
- Avoid common mistakes that stall or sidetrack healthcare entrepreneurs

This isn't about rushing. It's about moving with *intention* and having a roadmap to help you stay focused and flexible as you build.

Your Next Step

This is your invitation to lean in. To get curious. To explore boldly.

You already carry the heart of a healer and the mindset of a problem solver. Now, you're about to uncover the idea that ties it all together. Let's discover it together.

Chapter 10

Serving Your First Clients

Once you see yourself clearly in this role, the next critical step is to find the people who need you most. This means diving deep into your community to understand who they are, what challenges they face, and how you can make a meaningful difference in their lives.

Know Your Community: Start by researching the demographics of your area. Are there seniors living alone? Patients with chronic illnesses who struggle to get to a clinic? Families overwhelmed by caregiving responsibilities? Understanding these pain points will help you tailor your services to meet real needs.

Create Pathways for Connection: How will these potential clients find you? Word-of-mouth is powerful, especially in healthcare, but it often starts with intentional outreach. Here are several strategies to consider:

- **Build Partnerships with Local Agencies:** Reach out to home health agencies, social workers, hospice programs, senior centers, and assisted living facilities. Share your services and explain how you complement their work. For example, I connected with home health agencies where I had worked previously these relationships became key referral sources.
- Network with Other Healthcare Providers: Attend local medical society meetings, join nurse practitioners or physician assistant groups, or connect with hospital discharge planners. Let them know what services you provide so they can refer patients who need care.
- Community Engagement: Volunteer to speak at local events, senior centers, or faith-based organizations. Hosting informational sessions or health fairs can introduce you directly to your target population and their families. I would host free health seminars at senior centers and hand out flyers about my practice.
- Use social media and Online Platforms: Establish a professional online presence where you share educational content about the benefits of your services like home-based care, as well as patient testimonials or case studies (you can use pseudonyms). Even simple posts can raise awareness and lead to inquiries.
- Leverage your Personal Networks: Don't overlook the people you already know. Friends, family, former colleagues, or neighbors can be your first clients or can connect you with someone in need.

A Story from My Early Days:

My first patients mostly came through word of mouth. Hospital discharge planners who identified patients with frequent rehospitalizations or those without an established primary care provider became a steady and valuable referral source for me. I also began telling everyone I knew that I had started seeing patients at home, particularly those who needed primary care but couldn't leave their homes due to physical, cognitive, or other limitations. My biggest momentum came from my connections within the assisted and personal care communities. These relationships helped me identify many unmet needs among current and pending residents.

Many of these individuals were new to the area and had not yet established care with a primary care provider. Meanwhile, they were already packed up and in route or even waiting in the parking lot of the assisted living community, ready to move in. Without even initially planning to, I found myself providing valuable service by meeting these patients right where they were, whether that was their new residence, a hotel room, a neighbor's living room, or a community center. Any agreed upon space became a trusted meeting place for delivering care.

Serve Them Well:

Once you have your first clients, the way you serve them will shape your reputation and future success. Listen closely to their stories, needs, and concerns. Every visit is an opportunity to learn and improve your care approach. Be responsive, compassionate, and professional; it's these qualities that build lasting trust.

Remember, your first clients are not just customers, they are your foundation. Their experiences will become your testimonials, your referrals, and the heart of your growing practice.

Top Tip #1: Draw on Your Experience

Where Passion Meets Purpose

When it comes to launching a healthcare business, it's easy to get caught up in the idea that you have to create something entirely new, something groundbreaking and never before seen. But the truth is, one of your most powerful tools is something you already have: your lived experience.

Think about your day-to-day work in healthcare.
What are the moments that energize you?
What types of clients do you connect with most naturally?
What situations make you think, *"If only someone would fix this..."*?

That someone might be you.

Throughout my own journey, I realized that many of my best business decisions were rooted not in elaborate strategy but in reflection. I paid attention to the things I did naturally and the problems I found myself returning to, time and time again.

For example, long before I launched my home-based primary care practice, I had years of experience in home health care as a registered nurse in the field, as a clinical manager, as a branch director, and eventually as an area director. I saw firsthand how underserved our elderly, homebound, and rural populations were. It wasn't a passing observation, it was a pattern.

Families were overwhelmed. Patients couldn't access care. Providers were too far removed. I knew the system was broken in that space and over time, I stopped waiting for someone else to fix it. I became the fix.

I didn't stumble across my idea by accident.
I lived it. I saw it. I felt it. And eventually, I decided to do something about it.

Start With What You Know

If you're looking for the right idea, start by asking yourself these questions:

- What part of your current role excites you the most? Is it educating families? Coordinating complex care? Advocating for underserved populations?
- What problems are you constantly bumping into? Are clients falling through the cracks, are patients underserved because no one is available for follow-up care? Are older adults in your region waiting weeks or months for basic services?
- What unmet needs do your clients have in aesthetic services or wellness? For example, are they struggling to maintain results between treatments? Do they need guidance on skincare routines or wellness plans? Are some services hard to access or confusing to navigate?

- What would you do all day if money weren't a concern? That's a powerful clue toward your zone of genius, the work that feels purposeful, fulfilling, and naturally aligned with your strengths. Personally, I never started my business with the goal of getting rich. In fact, I often say,

    "If I were in it for the money, I'd be doing something else." For me, it was always about service, meeting a need, solving a problem, and showing up for the people who needed care the most

These questions help reveal the natural next step in your career, the place where your passion and experience intersect with a *real need in your community*.

This is where your best business ideas live.

When you draw on what you've already seen, done, and loved, you build a business that's authentic, sustainable, and grounded in deep insight. You'll be serving people whose challenges you understand, because you've been there. You know their pain points. You've had the conversations, you've walked hospital halls, entered patients' homes, and met clients where they are and you've answered those difficult calls, held those family meetings.

And because of that - you're already ahead.

The Power of Alignment

When your business is aligned with your professional experience and your personal passion, it becomes more than just a job, it becomes a calling. You'll show up differently. You'll market more confidently. You'll lead with a clarity that only comes from being deeply connected to your *why*.

And perhaps most importantly, you'll be trusted because people know when they're dealing with someone who *gets it*.

This doesn't mean you have to have all the answers. But it does mean you're starting from a place of truth. And that matters more than any business degree or startup checklist.

Ready to Go Deeper?

Now that you've looked inward and started identifying your natural strengths and calling, the next step is to look outward.

In the next chapter, we'll explore how to spot the real problems your future clients are facing, the unmet needs, the hidden frustrations, and the opportunities for you to step in as the solution.

Let's keep building.
Because the people you're meant to serve?
They're already out there waiting for you to see them.

Chapter 11

Seeing What's Missing: Creating What's Next

Now that you've reflected on your own experience, it's time to shift your focus outward to the problems and gaps you encounter every day as a healthcare professional.

Because building a purposeful and sustainable business isn't just about what *you* want to do. It's also about identifying *what others need* and what they may not even realize they're missing.

In my case, this meant recognizing gaps I had been seeing for years. Working in home healthcare exposed me to challenges that repeated like clockwork: patients with no access to consistent primary care, delayed treatment because of lack of follow-up, overburdened family caregivers with no one to guide them, and organizations desperate for a provider to help close the loop in transitional care.

These were not theoretical problems. These were real people falling through real cracks and no one was stepping in.

That's when I realized: *maybe I was the one meant to step in.*

Top Tip #2 – Identify Gaps

Look For Where the System Falls Short

You don't have to search far to find gaps in healthcare. In fact, most of them are hiding in plain sight. If you're a nurse, clinician, or allied health professional, chances are you've already seen dozens of opportunities for improvement.

But here's the shift: instead of just noticing those issues, start asking yourself *why* they exist and *what could be done differently.*

Ask yourself:

- What problems do I see repeatedly?
- What unmet needs keep patients, families, or teams stuck?
- What delays care, complicates outcomes, or causes unnecessary stress?
- Is there a better, simpler, more compassionate way to address it?

These questions are where true innovation is born.

What Delays Care

In my work, I've seen how small barriers can snowball into serious health consequences. Transportation, for example, remains a major obstacle. A 72-year-old stroke survivor missed two critical follow-up appointments because his daughter worked full-time and had difficulty taking time off to transport him. The only non-emergent transport options in his area had limited hours and required booking days in advance. By the time he was referred to me and I conducted an assessment, his blood pressure had climbed to dangerous levels. Because he had missed his appointments, his medications were not refilled, a step normally handled during a follow-up clinic visit. This oversight put him at serious risk for another stroke.

Sometimes delays aren't just about getting to an appointment, they're also about getting the green light for care. One 54-year-old woman with worsening knee pain waited over a month for insurance approval for an MRI to establish a treatment plan. By the time she finally had the scan, her mobility had declined so much that she now relied on a walker, something early intervention might have prevented. Her limited mobility made attending follow-up clinic visits difficult, and without follow-up, an order for the physical therapy she needed could not be generated. Thankfully, she was referred to me, and under my care through home-based primary care, I was able to order physical therapy to help intercept further decline.

Lack of timely follow-up is another gap I see frequently. After a hospital discharge for heart failure, one patient went 18 days without being seen by a provider due to challenges leaving her home. During that time, no one had checked her weight or adjusted her medications both key to managing her symptoms. In less than a week, she was back in the ER, facing a severe flare-up of her heart failure.

Even when appointments happen, communication breakdowns can derail progress. I recall one patient whose discharge summary was faxed to the wrong clinic. His new provider didn't know his medications had been changed, and unknowingly doubled his dose for three days.

And then there's the long wait to see specialists. In many cases, getting to a specialist requires a referral from a primary care provider. For patients who have difficulty leaving their home, even securing that initial referral can be a challenge. Those extra steps create delays that put them at risk of missing the window for timely diagnosis and treatment.

The Opportunity in the Gaps

Each of these situations represents a place where care was delayed, disrupted, or derailed. For every barrier, there's an opportunity for a provider to step in, bridge the gap, and prevent harm. That's where you, as an independent clinician, as an entrepreneur and problem solver can become the difference.

Identifying gaps isn't about pointing fingers, it's about spotting the places where the system falters and asking, *What can I do here?* Sometimes, your role is as simple as making a follow-up call within 48 hours, doing a medication review, or offering an in-home assessment. Small actions in the right moments can completely change the trajectory of a patient's health.

The more you notice these patterns and act on them, the more you'll position yourself as a trusted problem-solver and the more patients, families, and healthcare partners will turn to you first.

The Clues Are in the Conversations

One of the most powerful tools you have as a future entrepreneur is your ability to *listen*. Every complaint, every "I wish," and every moment of patient or provider frustration is a clue.

For me, the turning point came during conversations with hospital case managers, hospice teams, and home health agencies. They'd mention patients who couldn't be discharged safely because they didn't have a primary care provider. Or families trying to move into assisted living but stuck because they had no provider to complete a pre-admission assessment or medication reconciliation.

It was so consistent it became undeniable.

> One of the most common situations I encountered early on was getting calls from assisted living communities about a pending resident relocating from out of state. These individuals were often still navigating the challenges of establishing care with a local provider. Time was always of the essence. They had already paid their deposit, their medications were sometimes in limbo because of crossing state lines, or they had experienced an unexpected injury during travel that now required medical attention.
>
> The conversations often revealed that the team wasn't sure how best to navigate these challenges. Without a primary care provider established, there was no one to complete the required pre-admission assessment or to address urgent health concerns. This uncertainty created anxiety for both the resident and their families, especially knowing that the

assisted living placement could be lost if the process took too long.

These episodes of frustration became all too familiar. I had heard the same story before, almost word for word, from other community directors and care coordinators. Sometimes it was a man who had driven down to Georgia with his daughter and needed a medication refill before move-in. Other times it was a couple who had sold their home and arrived with nothing but suitcases, boxes and a list of unaddressed health concerns from the move.

It happened so often it was impossible to ignore, this was a clear, recurring gap in the primary care system. People were falling between the cracks during one of the most vulnerable transitions of their lives and I realized I could be the one to fill that gap.

I realized I wasn't just seeing gaps. I was invited to fill them.

And so, I did.

From Overlooked to Opportunity

I began offering services specifically designed to meet these missed needs. I partnered with agencies I'd previously worked with. I leaned on my clinical experience and used it to create bridges where there had once been barriers.

One of the most rewarding surprises in this journey came in the form of unexpected phone calls like a former colleague who once reported to me, now reaching out as a partner eager to work together again, or an administrator who had moved on to another assisted living community calling to say, "I remembered what you did for us before, and I knew we had to bring you in here." Moments like that stopped me in my tracks. It was humbling to know that the care I had provided had left such a lasting impression and validating to see those relationships come full circle. Together, we weren't just reconnecting, we were weaving together a continuum of care that simply hadn't existed before.

My business wasn't built on a grand innovation.

It was built on a simple truth: *I paid attention.*

Gaps Are Your Goldmine

Don't underestimate the power of your clinical insight. You are uniquely positioned to spot inefficiencies, see what's missing, and understand what truly matters to the people you serve.

And the best part? When you build a business around solving these problems, you're not just creating a product, you're creating *impact*.

Your patients will feel it.
Your partners will see it.
Your community will thank you for it.

Identifying a gap is just the beginning. The next step is putting your idea into motion.

But before you invest time, money, or energy building a full-scale business, you need to test your idea quickly and strategically. That means:

- **Getting feedback early**
  Talk to potential clients, colleagues, or mentors to see if your idea solves a real problem. Be strategic about who you get feedback from, choose people whose insight is relevant and trustworthy. Early feedback helps you refine your concept before committing significant resources.

- **Avoiding common traps that stall healthcare entrepreneurs**
  Be aware of pitfalls like overbuilding your business too soon, underestimating regulations, or ignoring your target audience's real needs. Learning from others' mistakes can save time and money.

- **Making small moves that lead to big insight**
  Start with pilot programs, small experiments, or limited services to see what works. These incremental steps provide valuable data and direction for scaling your business effectively.

Clarity doesn't just come from thinking, it comes from *doing*.

In the next chapter, we'll explore how to test your idea with minimal risk and sidestep the costly mistakes that derail so many well-meaning entrepreneurs.

Let's keep moving—
Because the people you're meant to serve are already out there. And the solution they've been waiting for… might just be *you*.

From Inspiration to Execution: Build, Test, Collaborate

By now, you've done the hard, inward work, reflecting on your strengths, identifying your *why*, and pinpointing the very real gaps in your community. You've likely been inspired by ideas that feel aligned with your mission and experience.

Now, it's time to take action.

But not just any action, *smart*, strategic, and *purposeful* action.

This next step is where your vision meets reality. It's where planning turns into progress.

And the key? Start small. Move fast. Partner wisely.

Top Tip #3 – Test Your Ideas Quickly & Identify Partnerships

Test Before You Scale

Here's the truth: You don't need a 5-year business plan to begin. You don't need a marketing firm, an office suite, or a big budget. What you do need is a willingness to test your idea quickly, and a readiness to learn as you go.

The goal here is not perfection. It's progress.

Start with a minimum version of your offering:

- **Can you pilot your service with a small group?**
  For example, offer your new service, whether it's home visits, chronic disease management, or telehealth to a small group of patients in your community or clinic. This allows you to see how your approach works in real life and gather valuable feedback to refine your care.

- **Can you run a limited-time trial to gauge demand?**
  Consider offering free or discounted appointments, virtual sessions, or educational workshops for a limited

period. Track participation, patient satisfaction, and outcomes to understand interest and impact before fully launching.

- **Can you offer your service informally to trusted clients or colleagues and ask for honest feedback?**
Invite former patients, friends, or healthcare colleagues to try out your service such as a pilot patient education class or an informal assessment visit and encourage them to share candid thoughts on what worked well and what could improve.

These simple steps let you test and improve your healthcare service without heavy upfront costs or complex plans, helping you build confidence and prove value one patient or session at a time.

This strategy lets you gather rapid feedback and make smarter decisions sooner, or even better, learn quickly without overcommitting your resources. It allows you to refine and adjust before investing time, money, and energy into something that might need a pivot.

It also builds something else: your confidence.

You'll gain clarity not just from brainstorming, but from action from watching how your ideas work in the real world and evolving in real time.

You Don't Have to Do It Alone

Entrepreneurship is often romanticized as a solo journey, but the truth is: *no one builds anything of substance alone.*

That's why, just as important as testing your idea, is identifying strategic partnerships, those individuals and organizations that can walk beside you, extend your reach, and elevate your impact.

Think of the proverb:
If you want to go fast, go alone. If you want to go far, go together.

This wisdom has never been truer than in healthcare entrepreneurship.

The Power of Strategic Partnerships

When I launched my own home-based primary care practice, one of the most game-changing decisions I made was to lean into my relationships. I tapped into a web of people I had worked with for years, home health agencies, hospice organizations, case managers, and fellow clinicians.

These weren't just colleagues. They became collaborators.
They became extensions of the care I provided.
They became *my village*.

So, look around you:

- Which organizations align with your mission?
- Who in your community is already serving the population you want to reach?
- Who benefits when you succeed?

These are your potential partners.

Your partnerships might include:

- Home health agencies looking for providers to co-manage care plans.
- Hospice teams needing a primary care bridge when patients transition.
- Mobile diagnostic services to support your in-home visits.
- Senior living communities that need assessments and medication reconciliation to facilitate move-ins.
- Faith-based or nonprofit organizations serving underserved populations.
- Former colleagues who share your values and want to grow with you.

Don't underestimate the value of these connections. They can help fill service gaps, support your patients, and lend credibility to your businesses, especially in the early stages.

One of the best examples of this was when I hired longtime licensed practical nurse (LPN) and clinical partner LaRhonda, who had previously worked with me during my time as an registered nurse in home health care. LaRhonda quickly became my right hand as I built my practice, allowing me to focus more fully on patient care. Equally important, I brought on my long-time friend Shona to manage all the administrative functions of the office. Their invaluable support created the foundation that allowed the practice to run smoothly and efficiently.

You're the Orchestrator

Remember: *You don't have to do everything yourself.*

Your role is not to be the hero in every story, it's to be the orchestrator of care, the connector of people, and the curator of resources.

This mindset frees you to focus on what matters most: your patients, your mission, and your growth.

So, while you're out there testing your ideas, keep your eyes open for partners who complement what you do. The people you align with early on will influence the culture, the reach, and the sustainability of your business.

Build your team. Build your village.
Because the truth is, *you can't do it alone, and you don't have to.*

In Summary: Start Smart, Start Small, Start Connected

- Start testing your ideas with a small group to gain real-world insight.
- Keep it simple, refine your concept before scaling.
- Engage partnerships that share your values and expand your capabilities.
- Stay agile, curious, and open to change.

Testing and collaboration are not just early-stage strategies, they are lifelong habits of effective business leaders.

Setting the Stage for Growth: Embracing the Next Level

Congratulations, you've taken the bold step to start your healthcare business. That alone is a huge achievement, and you deserve to celebrate it. But now, let's talk about what comes next, the exciting and sometimes challenging journey of growth.

Starting small means you've focused on launching and learning quickly. You've tested your ideas, found your first clients, and carved out your niche. Now, the next phase is about building on that foundation and expanding your impact.

Champagne Problems: Good Challenges to Have

Growth brings new kinds of challenges, ones I like to call "champagne problems." These are the complex, rewarding issues that mean you're succeeding, scaling, and making a bigger difference. They might feel overwhelming at times, but they're signs you're on the right path.

Some of these challenges might include:

- Managing a growing team and learning how to lead effectively
- Balancing patient care with administrative duties and business strategy
- Navigating financial decisions like budgeting for new hires or equipment
- Expanding your services or entering new markets while maintaining quality
- Building systems and workflows that keep your practice running smoothly

Each of these represents a step forward, a chance to refine your leadership skills, clarify your vision, and deepen your commitment to your patients and community.

Leadership: The Heart of Sustainable Growth

At this stage, leadership moves to the forefront. It's no longer just about your individual skills as a clinician or entrepreneur. It's about inspiring and guiding others, creating a shared mission, and building a culture that supports everyone's success.

Leadership isn't just a title or position, it's a mindset. It's about:

- Listening deeply to your team and your patients
- Making tough decisions with empathy and integrity
- Encouraging innovation and continuous learning
- Setting boundaries to protect your time and energy
- Celebrating successes, big and small, to keep morale high

Strong leadership will help you not only manage growth but thrive through it, keeping your business aligned with your core values.

Painting Your Future: Visualizing Success

Imagine your practice a year from now. Maybe you have a small team supporting you, a nurse, an office manager, a billing specialist. You're seeing more patients, offering new services, and deepening your community connections.

With that growth, you're solving problems faster and more creatively. Your patients trust you even more because you're available, responsive, and organized. You've built workflows that free you to focus on what matters most: compassionate, personalized care.

And yes, some days will be hectic. There will be moments of doubt or frustration. But those days will be outweighed by the joy of seeing your vision come to life, the gratitude from patients, and the knowledge that you're making a real difference.

As you stand on the threshold of this next chapter, remember that growth is not a finish line, it's a continuous journey. Each challenge you face is an opportunity to sharpen your leadership, strengthen your practice, and deepen your impact. Keep your passion at the core, lean on your support system, and embrace the inevitable twists and turns with grace.

Now, with this foundation laid out and your vision clear, you're ready to step forward boldly. Lead with passion. Serve with purpose. Your journey is just beginning and the impact you'll make is waiting on the other side of your next step.

Conclusion
Lead with Passion. Serve with Purpose

As you close this book and prepare to launch or grow your own healthcare business, remember this:

Lead with your passion and always put people first.
You are the answer to the problem you identified. That truth is powerful. It means you have what it takes to make a difference. Your unique skills, your empathy, and your commitment position you to fill a gap in care that others may overlook.

But you don't have to do it alone. Surround yourself with the right resources, people who believe in your vision, mentors who guide you, and networks that support your growth. These relationships will be your anchors in uncertain times and your springboard when opportunities arise.

You won't have all the answers right away and that's okay. In fact, embracing uncertainty is part of the journey. Get comfortable with hearing "no," with failure, and with things not unfolding exactly as you planned. I learned along the way that it was often the moments when things didn't go as intended that pushed me to adapt, innovate, and ultimately build a stronger, more resilient business.

There is no straight path in entrepreneurship. Your business will develop and evolve as you listen carefully to your market, respond to feedback, and stay open to change. Flexibility isn't a weakness; it's a vital strength.

In 2018, I became the first Nurse Practitioner in my region to launch a home-based care practice as a solo practitioner. Today, several businesses have followed suit, offering similar services to serve this community and improve lives every day. This is incredibly validating, it confirms that I was on to something then, and you are too.

Keep moving forward with courage, clarity, and compassion. Celebrate the small wins and learn from the setbacks. Remember why you started and let that purpose fuel your persistence.

Your journey is just beginning and the impact you'll make is waiting on the other side of your next step. Take it.

The world needs your care, your voice, and your leadership now more than ever.

Reminder: Don't forget to download your free **Why Worksheet** to help turn your motivation into actionable steps. You can grab it at NursesMindYourBusiness.com

Connect with me and join the conversation on social media:

- **Facebook:** @NursesMindYourBusiness
- **LinkedIn:** @NursesMindYourBusiness
- **Instagram:** @NursesMindYourBusiness
- **TikTok:** @NursesMindYourBusiness

Your community, your resources, and your next steps are all just a click away, let's keep building this journey together.

References

American Medical Association. (n.d.). *CPT® (Current Procedural Terminology)*. https://www.ama-assn.org/practice-management/cpt

Centers for Medicare & Medicaid Services. (n.d.). *Medicare fee-for-service payment*. https://www.cms.gov/Medicare/Medicare-Fee-for-Service-Payment

Centers for Medicare & Medicaid Services. (n.d.). *National Provider Identifier Standard (NPI)*. https://www.cms.gov/Regulations-and-Guidance/Administrative-Simplification/NationalProvIdentStand

Chernew, M. E. (2011). Fee-for-service, accountable care organizations, and Medicare Advantage: Why? *Health Affairs, 30*(9), 1754–1760. https://doi.org/10.1377/hlthaff.2011.0778

Council for Affordable Quality Healthcare. (n.d.). *CAQH for providers*. https://www.caqh.org/providers

National Committee for Quality Assurance (NCQA). (n.d.). *What is Credentialing?* https://www.ncqa.org/programs/health-plan-credentialing/credentialing-overview/

Patel, R., & Sharma, S. (2025, January). *Credentialing*. In StatPearls [Internet]. Treasure Island, FL: StatPearls Publishing. Retrieved September 8, 2025, from https://www.ncbi.nlm.nih.gov/books/NBK519504/

Practice Solutions, LLC. (2022, July 5). *What is Availity and how is it helpful for insurance billing?* Practice Solutions. https://www.practicesol.com/single-post/what-is-availity-and-and-how-is-it-helpful-for-insurance-billing

My Journey

I want to take you on a journey that traces the path to where I am today.

I was born on the island of St. Croix, U.S. Virgin Islands, to Frederick and Zenia Raymond originally from the island of St. Lucia. I'm one of seven children, with five brothers and one sister. Early in life, I learned the value of family and community. I was raised in a household that deeply respected the elderly, and I had the fortune of growing up with the support and presence of both my maternal and paternal grandmothers. In a community where aunts and uncles served as trusted guides, they instilled in me a deep sense of pride, resilience, and the belief that hard work was not optional, it was expected.

In my community, older adults are honored and valued, a principle that would later shape the foundation of my career and passion.

My journey away from home began when I left St. Croix to attend the University of Maryland Eastern Shore on a volleyball scholarship. During my middle and high school years, I was fortunate to be introduced to the sport and mentored by my coach and longtime friend Ophelia Williams-Jackson; an experience that played a pivotal role in shaping my leadership skills.

Through volleyball, I learned far more than athletic technique. I discovered the value of teamwork, the importance of showing up for others, the strength of lasting friendships, and the power of commitment. These lessons would later echo through my personal and professional life.

While at the University of Maryland Eastern Shore, I earned a Bachelor of Science in Biology with a minor in Chemistry. Driven by a desire to serve others through healthcare, I went on to pursue and obtain my Master's degree in Physical Therapy, marking the official start of my journey in the healthcare field.

The transition from education to professional licensure wasn't without its challenges. Along the way, I was introduced to nursing. While I enjoyed my role as a physical therapist, I felt a pull, an inner nudge to do more, to engage more clinically, and to find a path that allowed broader impact. Nursing presented itself as that path, offering a robust and varied career. One that encompassed clinical care, education, and leadership opportunities that I hadn't even imagined at the time.

With that vision in mind, I returned to school and earned my Bachelor of Science in Nursing from the University of Alabama in Huntsville in 2003. Nearly 13 years later, I pursued advanced education once again, earning my Master of Science in Nursing and becoming a board-certified Adult-Gerontology Nurse Practitioner. My continued desire to expand my knowledge and elevate my professional impact led me to complete a Doctor of Nursing Practice at South University, with a focus on Leadership and Management. For my doctoral project, I examined how social determinants of health affect older adults, specifically focusing on the lack of transportation and its impact on managing chronic disease.

I share this roadmap not to list credentials, but to highlight the intentionality behind each step. None of this happened overnight. Each milestone represents a goal set, pursued, and achieved, always with the intention of giving back to my community and staying rooted in the values I was raised with: family, service, and honoring our elders.

My introduction to home health care came shortly after I became a registered nurse in 2003. Before that, I worked as an MDS coordinator in long-term care. That role became my first real connection to geriatric care, and I fell in love with it immediately. It reminded me of home, a culture where the elderly are respected, valued, and not overlooked.

That setting affirmed for me that aging does not diminish a person's worth. I learned that there's immense value in listening, in honoring the wisdom and life stories of those who came before us. Even as a clinician, I remained a student, eager to learn from the lives of my patients.

When I moved from Alabama to Maryland, I began working as a home health nurse with Peninsula Home Health Care in Salisbury, MD. This experience solidified my calling. I discovered a level of autonomy and responsibility that deeply appealed to me. I had the privilege of working with a clinical manager, Susie, who helped me build strong foundational skills. Everything from wound care and wound vacs to phlebotomy and IV therapy. In home health, nurses often manage complex cases independently, and I thrived in that environment.

That time as a home health nurse shaped me. It gave me confidence. It gave me purpose. When I relocated back to Alabama, I continued in home health and eventually carried that work with me into Georgia. Each stage of this journey kept me closely tied to rural health and the older adult population, both areas that continue to be central to my clinical focus.

As my career progressed, I was given opportunities to transition from field registered nurse to leadership roles; first as a Clinical Manager, then Branch Director, and ultimately Area Director. These roles allowed me to blend my personal mission with my professional goals. Everything came full circle, the values instilled in me during my childhood on St. Croix, the discipline and a fierce work ethic taught to me by my mother and father, Frederick and Zenia Raymond, the guidance of my grandmothers Emelene Raymond and Roudette Jn-Batiste, the leadership skills I gained on the volleyball court under the mentorship of a coach and friend, and the loyalty forged within a tight-knit family of siblings Ronald, Francis, Yvette, Bill, Phil and Jason.

Each experience played a part in shaping who I am today.

I take none of it for granted. I believe every chapter of my journey has unfolded with purpose. And I believe that nothing happens before its time.

As I look to the future, I remain committed to growing educationally, professionally, and personally. I continue to seek opportunities to mentor others, to expand my reach, and to create environments that feel safe, welcoming, and compassionate for patients, families, and colleagues alike.

As providers, we often forget that while we are familiar with the medical world, our patients are not. For a family navigating a loved one's dementia diagnosis, or adjusting to life in assisted living, this is unfamiliar, often overwhelming terrain. There's no handbook for these life changes. That's where we come in. It's not just about being knowledgeable, it's about being kind, present, and empathetic.

I made a promise to this profession a long time ago. That promise includes showing up with compassion, not judgment. It includes recognizing that new nurses deserve mentorship just like I received from Susie in Maryland. If she hadn't taken the time to teach and guide me, I may have walked away from this field.

I'm grateful I didn't.

I'm excited about what comes next. And I hope that through this book, you've caught a glimpse of my heart, not just as a clinician, but as a wife, a mother, a daughter, a sister, and a friend. It's an honor to share this journey with you. If you find yourself drawn to a path like mine, I hope this story reminds you that the journey may be long, but it's always worth it.

www.ingramcontent.com/pod-product-compliance
Lightning Source LLC
Chambersburg PA
CBHW070637030426
42337CB00020B/4047